A ***WESTERN HORSEMAN*** BOOK

THE HISTORY OF WESTERN HORSEMAN

75 Years of the World's Leading Horse Magazine

By Randy Witte

Edited by Fran Devereux Smith

Western Horseman

Published by
WESTERN HORSEMAN magazine
2112 Montgomery St.
Fort Worth, TX 76107
817-737-6397

www.westernhorseman.com

Design, Typography and Production
Globe Pequot Press
Guilford, Connecticut

Printing
Lake Book Manufacturing Inc.
Melrose Park, Illinois

Printed in the United States of America

First Printing: May 2011

ISBN 978-0-7627-7753-2

DEDICATION AND ACKNOWLEDGMENTS

This book is dedicated to all the readers, writers, advertisers and other contributors to The World's Leading Horse Magazine since 1936.

Special thanks go to Marsha, my loving wife and partner, who has helped and supported me in so many ways throughout our 40 years together. Thanks also to our daughter, Mary Claire Niemeyer, who with Marsha helped to bring me through serious illness while I was working on this book.

Grateful appreciation goes to Chan Bergen, Pat Close and Gary Vorhes, for their recollections and proofreading; to JoAnne Spencer Clark and her daughters Barbara Jo and Debra, for sharing their memories of Dick Spencer; to Karan Miller, who provided a lot of history and photos that might otherwise have been overlooked; to Jonathan L. Snow and the John Ben Snow Foundation, for information and photos on JBS; and to Fran Smith, former colleague and now *Western Horseman* books publishing director, who helped with the final editing and photo selection.

Thanks also to those current *Western Horseman* staff members who explained how the magazine is published today. They include Darrell Dodds, publisher; Ernie King, associate publisher; and Ross Hecox, editor.

Finally, thanks to my mother, N. Jean Witte, who with my late father, Erwyn E. Witte, started a savings account for the Witte kids so they could buy their first horse. I'm also grateful to my in-laws, the late Mike and Mary Stees, who took me under wing and taught me about ranching and raising horses and cattle.

This book has focused mainly on editorial staff members at *Western Horseman* through the years. The editorial department is the "face" of the magazine to most readers, and I was part of it and therefore most familiar with it. This does not mean the advertising, circulation and business departments were not important to me. I simply wrote what I knew best, and if there are any *Western Horseman* staffers out there, past or present, who feel I slighted them in this book, I assure you it was unintentional.

WELCOME

The fact that you're reading this book suggests you're passionate about horses, or magazines, or, in the best of all possible worlds, both. Odds are, you're familiar with *Western Horseman* magazine either as a casual reader or perhaps as one of the faithful who began reading your folks' copy; you might have even introduced the magazine to your own kids.

Regardless of the reason you picked up this book, I assure you that your time on these pages will be well spent. The history of *Western Horseman* is a unique story, one that began with the simple vision of one man, Paul Albert, who desired to publish a periodical "to promote the use of the Western Horse and to assist the rider in all of his problems connected with his horse."

It's a shame Albert didn't live long enough to see his magazine flourish, nor to see the horsemanship revolution his little magazine has inspired. Today, Western riding has become an international pursuit, with stock-horse competitions held on every continent. Attend this country's top stock-horse events and you're sure to find competitors from around the globe who have been influenced by *Western Horseman* magazine.

I'm often asked why *Western Horseman* has been so successful for such a long period of time. The simple answer is this: The magazine never has been overly impressed by trends or fads; it has never strayed from its original purpose. In a day and age of celebrity worship, when every magazine on the newsstand appears to feature the same people on the covers, *Western Horseman* remains dedicated to telling the stories of the real men, women, horses, associations and events that make up the stock-horse universe.

In addition, this magazine always has been produced by people who own, ride, train and care for horses. Dick Spencer, the legendary editor and publisher, once said that if you know the reader, you can figure out everything else. As a dyed-in-the-wool horseman, Spencer knew what the reader wanted, and he supplied it on every page during his long career with the magazine.

Former *Western Horseman* Publisher Randy Witte has authored the most comprehensive history of the magazine ever written. In reality, no other person could tell the story as objectively and accurately. Witte joined the *Western Horseman* staff during its "cut-and-paste" days and guided the magazine into the modern world of desktop publishing. Although never a computer whiz, he recognized the need to stay current with technology and invested in equipment and training when it was needed most.

Witte also recognized that a magazine, when done well, can be magical in its ability to educate, inform, entertain and inspire. He continued the traditions established by his predecessors, giving the magazine an addictive quality. People have returned issue after issue, year after year, to read articles or columns by their favorite writers or to laugh at the humor of their favorite cartoonists. The magazine has been made for a community of like-minded individuals, who use *Western Horseman* as a means of escape to an exciting world fueled by their passion for horses.

"Our goal at *Western Horseman* was to take the readers to places they'd never go," said Witte, "meet interesting characters they'd never heard of and learn things they'd never imagined."

As we celebrate *Western Horseman*'s 75th Anniversary, we face new challenges brought on by a technological revolution that is changing every facet of our business. Although the vast majority of current *Western Horseman* readers prefer the convenience, portability and tactile experience of reading a print magazine, many newcomers to the magazine are demanding access on multiple platforms and want our content on an "on-demand" basis. Rather than relying on still images alone to tell our stories, we now are capturing video and sound at westernhorseman.com to provide a much richer and interactive experience.

Where will all of this lead? To be honest, we have no earthly idea. What we do know is that, regardless of the technology employed, we will continue educating, inspiring and informing our audience in the best *Western Horseman* tradition.

Darrell Dodds, publisher

PREFACE

The colorful story behind one of the oldest and most successful magazines in the world — *Western Horseman*, founded in 1936.

I discovered *The Western Horseman* magazine as a youngster when I walked into a drug store one summer day in the early 1960s, looking for a comic book on the newsstand. The comics were displayed on one end of that stand, but I never got to them. Instead, a bright yellow banner behind black type on one of the magazine covers proclaimed *The Western Horseman,* and it depicted a pleasant scene with horses and cowboys. The magazine was quickly in my hands and I never bought another comic book after that. Thumbing through the magazine, I knew I'd found something special, a real link to the world of horses and cowboys, ranching and rodeo. I knew this was the life for me, but the closest I'd come to it, up to then, was through a plethora of Westerns on television and at the movies, and with the backyard horse our family had recently acquired in Lakewood, Colo., just west of Denver.

A single copy of the magazine at that time cost 50 cents, but a one-year subscription offered 12 issues for $5. I had that much saved up from mowing lawns, and I sent it in. The issues arrived each month after that, and they were chock-full of the information I needed — all the latest news on the top rodeo cowboys, stories on trail riding and ranching, tips on equine health care, and training articles. That first year, with the magazine opened and lying at the edge of the corral, I taught our gentle bay mare, Spicy, how to back, and then how to pull a buggy. It was all there in the magazine, plus a lot more. *The Western Horseman* seemed like family — it was fun to follow the firsthand accounts of the folks in the editorial department as they participated in various rodeos, rides, brandings and so forth.

The man who seemed to head it all up was Dick Spencer III, who was listed as editor in those days. His enthusiasm for most everything that had to do with the American West and its rich history, particularly of cowboys, Indians and mountain men, showed through to the readers, and the readers got a steady diet of such history, along with the rest of the editorial mix, and liked it. In those days, I never dreamed of becoming a part of the magazine, but years later I was fortunate to embark on a long and enjoyable career with *The Western Horseman.* I worked with most of the people I'd read in earlier times, including Dick, who really was "bigger than life."

Looking back on it now, it's easy to see how the magazine nurtured me in many ways, not the least of which was providing an interesting career in the magazine business and a living for my family. Through the magazine, I learned that Colorado State University had a rodeo club, and that helped me decide to attend college there, where I enrolled in the journalism program and met my future wife, Marsha Stees, a ranch girl from Steamboat Springs.

I'll never forget how the magazine came through for me in my magazine article writing class at CSU. The idea was to learn how to come up with an article idea, then write it, query a magazine, and hopefully get the magazine to buy the article. You guessed it — I queried *The Western Horseman* about a story on "Judging Rodeo Bucking Events," and interviewed three top cowboys — Jim Houston, Jim Wise and Freckles Brown — on what they looked for when they took a turn serving as rodeo judges for bareback, saddle bronc, and bull riding. The class was nearly over for the quarter when I got the letter of acceptance from Barbara Emerson, secretary for Editor Chuck King. I showed it to the teacher and watched him get out his grade book and mark an A next to my name.

Years later, when I mentioned the incident to my boss, Chan Bergen, who was editor at that time, Chan remarked: "In other words, we saved your butt!" Records show I was paid $45 for the article, which appeared in the June 1969 issue.

While attending college, I became thoroughly steeped in rodeo and much of my life revolved around the CSU rodeo club. I tried bareback riding and was hopeless for that event, but enjoyed limited success in bull riding, which is still my favorite event to watch. Early on, it was apparent that my original idea of being a rodeo *writer* rather than *rider* was the way to go. I could have become a full-time reporter for *The Denver Post*. The door was opened to me for that position while still in college, and I enjoyed working a couple summers and holidays at the *Post* under the watchful eye of John Snyder, a friend and neighbor who got me hired as part-time copy boy and part-time reporter. I wound up filling in for vacationing reporters not only on the city desk, but also in county court and at the police department.

Red Fenwick, a popular *Post* columnist and reporter, befriended me and pulled some strings that resulted in a plush assignment one summer, covering the big Cheyenne Frontier Days Rodeo in Wyoming. Red was a cowboy at heart, a true Westerner and the only guy who wore a cowboy hat and boots to work at the *Post*. But I also had developed close ties to the Denver-based Rodeo Cowboys Association, particularly with Dave Stout, who was editor of the *Rodeo Sports News* at the time, and destined to become secretary-treasurer of the association.

Dave said there was an opening in the R.C.A.'s publicity department, a one-man and one-secretary operation, and I was hooked for good with a journalism job in pro rodeo. I had a tough time telling John Snyder I was foregoing a job with a prestigious big-city newspaper to become a rodeo publicist, but it turned out to be the right decision for me. After spending seven years with what became the Professional Rodeo Cowboys Association, I turned again to *The Western Horseman*, sending in a job application to Dick Spencer. Nearly a year went by, and I never heard a word from Dick or anyone else at the magazine. And then there was an opening at the magazine for someone who could write knowledgeably about rodeo. Chan Bergen offered me the job!

It's been said that people who really like their jobs can always remember the exact date they started work. For me it was October 3, 1977, when I walked through the front door of the Spanish-style office on North Nevada Avenue in Colorado Springs. The staff, I soon learned, was like a family, too. Dick was the undisputed patriarch, the consummate joke-teller who made coffee breaks social events not to be missed, and he was the glue that kept everything in place right up to his death in 1989. There were characters among us, and yes, we had family squabbles. But my intention with this book is to share the history of *The Western Horseman*, one of the oldest magazines in existence, and to recall a lot of the good times we had, some of the challenges we overcame, and to offer a glimpse into the lives of those who made it all work, especially during my tenure, which spanned 29 years.

In that time I started as editorial assistant, then worked as associate editor, editor, and finally as publisher. I saw the magazine go from typewriters to, reluctantly, a state-of-the-art computer system. We always seemed to drag our feet when new technology knocked at the door, but that wasn't always a bad thing. Along the way, we informed and entertained readers to the point that many of them included a visit to our office with their vacation plans. And we always received plenty of letters telling us what they liked or didn't like about the magazine. We were a part of so many of our readers' lives that it wasn't unusual to even get a letter now and then explaining why a certain longtime subscriber had failed to renew his subscription— the man had died and his widow wanted to let us know.

For the record, *The Western Horseman* was founded with the January 1936 issue. But it became simply *Western Horseman* beginning with the June 1982 issue. Why? Dick Spencer walked through the editorial offices one day, as he did every day, and glanced down at a future magazine cover being assembled on the cut-and-paste table. "You know," he said, "that word 'The' in the title really doesn't contribute anything. Why not just drop it and we'll go by *Western Horseman* from now on." And that explains the subtle name change. Dick could do that. He was the boss and there was no need for a consensus of opinion, board meeting, or any other nonsense. It was not until sometime later we thought to get the new name copyrighted!

Randy Witte

CONTENTS

1. Paul Albert 8

2. John Ben Snow 18

3. Dick Spencer 30

4. The 1950s 40

5. More Growth 50

6. The 1970s 66

7. In and Out of the Office 80

8. "As the World Turns" 92

9. The "Roaring" '90s 106

10. Into the 21st Century 122

Appendix 138

Index 154

Author Profile 159

VOL. 1   JANUARY, 1936   NO. 1
Subscription Price $ 1.00 per year   Single Copy 30 cents

The Western Horseman

In this issue
Review of
THE LAFAYETTE SHOW

1

PAUL ALBERT

The Man Who Started It

Paul Albert ran the idea past his wife, Worth. He wanted to create a horse magazine for owners and admirers of western horses, he said, for people who still wanted to ride and breed good horses that could be used for everything from ranch work to rodeo and horse show competition. He would research and write articles for the publication, and sell subscriptions and advertising to pay for the printing.

That was in 1935, and the Alberts were trying to scratch out a living with horses and cattle on their small Tarantula Ranch nestled in a valley near Lafayette, Calif., about 20 miles east of San Francisco. The country as a whole was still trying to pull out of the Great Depression, so there wasn't a lot of money available to most folks. And never mind that horses already had been displaced in the cities by street cars and automobiles, and were now leaving farms by the thousands in the form of down-payments on tractors. Horses, at that time, weren't even popular as pets. A lot of horses were being sent straight to slaughter to be made into dog food. When Paul asked Worth Albert what she thought of his idea for a horse magazine, her first thought might have been, "You're crazy, Paul. Forget it." Instead, she encouraged him to pursue his dream.

Follow That Dream

"We had moved from a mountain cattle ranch in the famous Mother Lode Sierras near Yosemite National Park with a few head of white-face cattle and a string of nine mountain horses we planned to use for rental purposes until, finances permitting, we could enlarge our herd and concentrate on cattle," Worth recalled nearly 20 years later.

Paul and Worth were frugal and optimistic, and weren't afraid to work. They hauled drinking water from a stream, used kerosene lamps for light, and during the week Paul often worked as a traveling salesman for tractors and other heavy equipment. Paul and Worth turned their place into a "one-day [Saturday] dude ranch," as they called it, where folks could ride, swap horse stories and stay for supper.

In an article written for the 50th anniversary issue of *Western Horseman* (January, 1986), author Peg Skorpinski also quoted Worth, who recalled: "Enthusiastic riders would economize all week to save 75 cents for an hour's ride, bring their lunches and stay all day, enjoying the outdoors, giving advice to other riders, and helping with the brushing, feeding, and saddling of horses. More and more the dudes wanted to stay for the evening, so I decided

The first issue of The Western Horseman *magazine was published in January 1936.*

Paul Albert, founder of The Western Horseman, *shows off the fish he caught at Tower Creek, Wyo., in 1931.*

to cook and serve dinners at cost—a big pot of beans with hot bread or a big meat loaf or stew and lots of coffee. We'd sing songs, play different instruments, and tell stories. Just a wonderfully good time, all for the big sum of about $1.10 each for all day, which included an hour's ride, supper, wine, and song."

Skorpinski described Paul as a tall, lanky redhead who was born in Indiana in 1902 and moved to California when he was 5 years old. He graduated from Berkeley High School in 1921, and his fellow students didn't remember him expressing any interest in horses. "It might be that his travels exposed him to the changing conditions of the working horse and he simply couldn't keep silent," she wrote.

Paul and Worth hired one employee, their friend Dorothy Smith, to help with typing. The first issue of the Alberts' new magazine came together in a modest wood cabin on the Tarantula Ranch, and cost $200 to print what was later described as an ambitious press run of 1,500 copies.

Paul is shown here with one of the Tarantula Ranch Arabians.

WESTERN HORSEMAN ARCHIVES

Volume 1

"January 1936, Volume 1, Number 1" appeared at the top of the first issue of *The Western Horseman* magazine, which was composed of 26 black-and-white pages measuring 7 x 10 inches and featured a photo of a glass-eyed horse on the cover. Subscription price was listed at $1 per year for the new quarterly magazine, and 30 cents per copy. Distribution of this first issue was designed to coincide with the first Lafayette Horse Show, also Paul's brainchild, and the show did help to get the magazine into the hands of a lot of future subscribers and advertisers. The modest little publication, printed on a shoestring budget, was to become the voice of a fledgling horse industry in the western United States and evolve into what was proudly proclaimed as the "World's Leading Horse Publication." Today, it still thrives as one of the oldest magazines in the country and the entire world.

In that first issue, P.T. Albert is listed as editor, and he and C.P. Raney, were named as owners. Raney was a friend who helped finance the magazine, until Paul was able to buy out the partnership the following year. Paul's enthusiasm for both equine history and for what he saw as a great, untapped future for horses is evident in the first and all the subsequent issues he published. In his opening editorial he began: "The art of

Worth Albert, second editor and owner of The Western Horseman, *with nephew Bob Keeney as a young cowboy at the ranch near Lafayette, California.*

Dorothy Smith stands in the doorway of The Western Horseman*'s first office, the ranch home of Paul and Worth Albert. The photo was taken in the mid-1980s.*

horsemanship is as old as the civilized human race. Almost coincident with the dawn of written history, our guide for the definition of civilization, man has been mounted on a horse....

"With the rapid advancement of transportation in the last twenty-five years, Americans have almost forgotten the qualities of horseflesh. Only a few of the older families in our country, whose traditions have followed the cattle business, have remained staunch adherents of the horse, both as a means of transportation and a valuable tool in the execution of work. In this industry the horse will always be indispensable.

"And as cattlemen have stuck with their horses while city dwellers have gone on to more rapid forms of travel, these same city dwellers have glanced back from time to time and been thrilled and pleased to see one group of people with their feet still in the stirrups. In recent years this thrill had recurred so often that certain of them have left the crowded pavements occasionally,

straddled a good old horse, and, strange as it seems, many for the first time in their lives, to discover that they have born into them a love for horses....

"We may fly, or sail, or glide over the roads on pneumatic tires with more comfort, but the love for good horseflesh will never be stamped out of humans while they still have red blood in their veins...."

The Light-Horse Family

The year 1936 saw Franklin Roosevelt in the third year of his presidency, the United States was still five years away from entering World War II, and there were but a handful of horse-breed registries, as outlined in Paul's first-issue assessment of the industry. "In the light-horse family," he wrote, "under which all saddle horses fall, several good breeds are represented in most sections, namely, the Thoroughbred, the Morgan, the Arabian and that class of colored horses we like to think of as the California breeds, such as the Palominos, Pintos and Buckskins."

Worth Albert is on her Arabian mare Mira at Tarantula Ranch, Lafayette, California. Peg Skorpinski gave this and other photos to Western Horseman *for the 50th anniversary. The pictures had been reproduced from the Albert photo album.*

In 1936, the Quarter Horse, today's most popular breed of horses, had not yet been identified as a breed, although some referred to this type of horse as a Steel Dust in honor of a legendary stallion by that name. But there were like-minded individuals, including many breeders, who were working on identifying and reproducing this type of horse that seemed to possess natural cow-savvy and athleticism, including quick bursts of speed over short distances. *The Western Horseman* would serve as a clearing-house of ideas among breeders, and a proponent for the formation of breed registries, not only for what became the Quarter Horse breed, but for other types of horses, too.

Recollections

Robert "Bob" Denhardt, another horse enthusiast, was a student at the University of California at Berkeley at this same time, and he quickly joined the Alberts in researching and writing about horses for the magazine. Paul asked Bob to research and write about the Steel Dust horses. Bob did so, and then went on to become an important founder and

The Western Horseman's *first employee, Dorothy Smith, her sister, Helen Minor (right), and Jim Allan, are shown during the early days at Tarantula Ranch. All are identified in the ranch album as "Tarantulaites—and how!"*
WESTERN HORSEMAN ARCHIVES

executive secretary of the American Quarter Horse Association, which formed in 1940. By that time, the magazine also had seen the successful formation of the Palomino Horse Association, the Appaloosa Horse Club and the Albino Horse Club, thanks in large part to Paul's urging in his editorials. Years later (September 1947 through August 1951), Bob Denhardt even served as editor of *The Western Horseman.*

In writing about the early years of the magazine, Bob recalled the following. "Paul was a horse historian, as well as an excellent horseman. His interest, knowledge, and personality had drawn to him a number of persons who were, or would become, well known in horse circles. Some examples are Dick Halliday, who founded the first Palomino horse association; George Glendenning, who got the Pinto horse rolling; Francis Haines, who was working on the Appaloosa horse; Luis Ortega, whose work with rawhide bosals, hackamores, and quirts was becoming widely known; Dan Coolidge, the western writer; Father Rivard, the Catholic regular who wrote under the name of Don Alfredo; and several others, including myself.

"Many a night we talked 'horse' until gray light began to show in the east. We all wrote for the early issues of *The Western Horseman,* contributing our talents to help Paul make the magazine popular and successful. The first issue of the magazine came out in January of 1936. In it was the first of a series of articles Paul wrote entitled 'Romance of the Western Stock Horse.' It is still one of the best historical surveys of the western horse. He spent a lot of time researching for the series, and I always thought it should be published in book form, and still do.

"Paul thought the *National Geographic* was the world's best magazine, and he followed its format in his magazine, in regard to both layout and type. He planned to balance the contents of the magazine with half editorial matter and half advertising—a format still generally followed today. But lack of ads

made such a division impossible in the early issues. In the editorial section he wanted the articles divided as evenly as possible between 'how to,' historical, and current events, such as shows, rodeos, ropings, etc. I wrote my first article for *WH* in the September 1936 issue. By the time I became editor some 11 years later, I had contributed at least 20 articles. My first check (for the fourth article) brought me five dollars. It was tough starting a magazine during the Depression."

An Unforeseen Move

Bob also noted that Paul had health problems in the years he knew him, though it wasn't apparent exactly what was bothering him. In October 1942, Paul died rather suddenly at the age of 40, and it was then

Here's a view of Tarantula Ranch at about the time The Western Horseman *began. Two buildings, two people, and a few head of cattle and horses comprised the ranch.*

Here's a shot of Tarantula Ranch in the late 1980s when development was a likely prospect in the future. The Alberts' nephew, Bob Keeney, had built everything at the headquarters except for the little white house partially obscured on the right.
WESTERN HORSEMAN ARCHIVES

determined he had been suffering from cancer. His was not an exceptionally long life, but he did live to see his magazine grow steadily along with the horse industry, and the future at that time looked very bright for readers and riders alike.

Worth Albert quietly took the reins as editor and publisher, and then she sold the magazine in 1943 to Speidel Newspapers Inc., whose majority stockholder was John Ben Snow, a dedicated horseman. The magazine was moved to the Speidel newspaper headquarters in Reno, Nev., and members of the Speidel staff were assigned positions in editorial and advertising. A new era was unfolding for *The Western Horseman,* and John Ben Snow would prove to be the right man at the right time to bring the magazine to new levels of greatness, ultimately in a new Colorado location.

2

JOHN BEN SNOW

The Benefactor

John Ben Snow led a long, colorful, and very successful life, and proved to be a great benefactor to *The Western Horseman,* financially and in other ways, at a time when the magazine was struggling. When the publication was moved to Reno in the year following Paul Albert's death, all files and related material fit easily in the trunk of Clarence Colbert's car. Clarence worked for Speidel in Reno. Shortly after the move, Speidel executives turned to Clarence and told him he would be the magazine's circulation director; another employee, Graham Dean, was told to assume the positions of editor and publisher. The next issue, however, listed Graham Dean only as publisher and Merrill Gaffney, another Speidel newspaperman, as editor. Despite their lack of horse knowledge, the Reno staff did a credible job in putting out the magazine every other month, but circulation was stagnant.

Financier and Quiet Advisor

John Ben Snow, or "JBS," as so many friends and associates referred to him, happened to settle in Colorado Springs after retiring from a long career

as an executive of the English management team of F.W. Woolworth Co., and their Five and Ten (cent) stores. Throughout his career, JBS opened a chain of Woolworth stores in Great Britain, and also enjoyed raising and riding horses for fox hunting, steeplechasing, and polo. Upon his retirement shortly before World War II, he returned to his native country, the United States, and eventually bought a ranch north of town, which was run by his foreman, Don Flint, who oversaw the horse and cattle operation. He had met Don and his wife, Florence, in Wyoming several years earlier, and they became great friends, ranch managers, and key figures in the evolution of the magazine.

One day, the story goes (according to the late Dick Spencer), JBS was musing to Don Flint about the magazine and said something like, "I wonder why we aren't doing better, why we aren't growing."

Without hesitation, Don said, "Well, the people running the magazine don't really know much about horses. You need to get some real horsemen involved."

The Western Horseman *office building, which was patterned after the Palace of the Governors in Santa Fe, N.M., is shown shortly after JBS had it built in 1949. The famous 14,110-foot Pikes Peak looms in the background.*

John Ben Snow brought The Western Horseman *to Colorado Springs in 1948. The photo was taken after JBS was retired from a successful career in England and comfortably settled in the Springs.*

WESTERN HORSEMAN ARCHIVES

Then, also without hesitation, JBS told Don he was now general manager of *The Western Horseman,* and asked that he put together a suitable staff. This was the last thing Don wanted to hear. He preferred working outdoors, especially with horses, and didn't relish the idea of spending much time in a magazine office. But he did as he was asked, and the magazine was moved to Colorado Springs in 1948 so JBS could keep a close eye on his "hobby" publication. JBS financed construction of the Spanish-style office, north of downtown, which also would boast a stable in back of the 5-acre lot, where traveling horsemen could overnight horses, and where members of *The Western Horseman* staff would keep horses at various times over the ensuing decades.

JBS played the role of financier and also quiet advisor who stayed in the background. His management style was to put good people in key positions, and then let them do their jobs. He was happy to comment on each issue of the magazine, which was hand-delivered to him at his downtown office, but he never dictated what should appear in the publication. JBS had three distinct phases of his life: his youth in New York, his years in Great Britain, and finally his years in Colorado Springs. He was such a big part of the magazine's continued success, a closer look at his entire life is warranted.

"JBS"

JBS was born June 16, 1883 in Pulaski, New York, according to his biographer and nephew, Vernon F. Snow, in his book *JBS, A Biography of John Ben Snow.* Much of the following material comes from the late Vernon Snow and his well-researched and well-written book. The Snow family can trace its roots to Elizabethan England, and to the Plymouth Plantation in 1624. Generation after generation shows a line of industrious, hard-working and successful people, village and church leaders, some with more money than others, but always with a sense of purpose combined with strong Christian values. At the time of his birth, John Ben Snow's parents were already middle-aged and he had one brother, who was 15.

JBS proved to be an enthusiastic student from the time he entered elementary school. He was short in stature (5' 5" as an adult), but excelled in track, baseball and football. He was also described as self-conscious and shy throughout most of his life. He was a lifelong bachelor. JBS also developed, early on, a keen interest in business and a desire to make his own way outside the boundaries of little Pulaski. He struck out on his own at age 19, found his way to New York City and the New York University, where he undertook a tremendous workload of studies, and was graduated with a bachelor's degree at age 21. Through church affiliations he became friends with the Rockefeller family, whom he looked upon as heroes worthy of his imitation.

In 1906, JBS took a job as stock boy in the basement of F.W. Woolworth's store on Manhattan's Sixth Avenue. Through hard work and a keen desire to excel in the business, he soon attracted attention from management and began his climb to the upper levels of the expanding Woolworth empire.

"The following year, at age 24," wrote Vernon Snow, "JBS transferred to Port Jervis, New York, to open a new Five and Ten store. There, in his first real management position, he proved his worth to the Woolworth dynasty. Located about 55 miles northwest of New York City along the banks of the Delaware River, Port Jervis was a bustling transportation hub in the first decade of the 20th century. JBS established a rapport with the community leaders, especially with Merritt C. Speidel, the editor of the *Port Jervis Daily Union,* the town's only newspaper. The store had a choice location in the middle of the downtown area. The newspaper provided the principal advertising medium. The customers supplied the nickels and dimes as JBS accumulated and deposited dollars in the bank and demonstrated his merchandising skill." He and Merritt Speidel would become lifelong friends, and that led to Snow's later investment in the Speidel newspaper chain.

Crossing the Pond

After opening variety stores throughout the United States, Woolworth's decided the time was right to expand into the British Isles. JBS jumped at the job he was offered—to help open new stores throughout England. "John Ben arrived in Liverpool on February 21, 1909, and took up residence at 25 Church Street," according to his biographer. "His first assignment was to assist in opening several new Woolworth stores in northern England.... At that time F.W. Woolworth and Co. Ltd. (comprised of Englishmen and Americans) consisted of the pioneer store in Liverpool and offices in London.

"In England, the Five and Ten-cent stores," Vernon Snow wrote, "were called Threepenny and Sixpenny stores. JBS was a master at buying good products and selling them at fair prices; and he especially enjoyed arranging grand openings. Three decades later, when JBS retired as a director of the British corporation and returned to America, there were 766 stores organized into three regional districts with thousands of employees and millions of British customers. He contributed greatly to the success of this enterprise; in fact, he made much of it possible."

During those years, when JBS made his fortune and became a major stockholder in his company, he grew to love English life, especially life in the country "and particularly such rural sports as horseback riding, fox hunting, polo, Thoroughbred breeding, and steeplechasing," wrote Vernon Snow. "He also acquired the traditional English fondness for all kinds of animals, especially horses. Thereafter the horse was JBS' first love."

He purchased a beautiful country estate, near Hertford, England, which he named Highfield Stud Farm. After JBS had been promoted in 1913 to buyer, an upper management position, he moved to London, the corporate headquarters. Friday afternoons would find JBS leaving his London home and driving some 30 miles in his Rolls Royce to Highfield for a weekend of entertaining friends and associates, with the main activities usually centered on polo. If weather was inclement, JBS had a mechanical horse in a shed at one end of his regulation-size polo field, where he would practice riding, swinging his mallet and hitting a ball.

"On weekends and holidays JBS, ever generous, opened the gates of Highfield and offered hospitality in the manner of an English squire or a knight of the shire," wrote Vernon Snow. "Small wonder that he soon acquired several new appellations. He remained JB to his secretary and most Woolworth associates. But to many country folk he became John B. Snow, *Esquire*—translated 'Squire Snow.' To his trainer George Beeby and his groom Maurice Head, he was 'the Guv'nor.' One American friend, Bill Feick, affectionately dubbed him 'Sir John,'" as if he'd been knighted.

As with everything in his life, JBS wanted to excel with his horses, and so it was no surprise he hired one of England's best trainers, Harry Beeby, and also Harry's son, George, who handled horse transportation to and from Highfield, played polo with JBS, and oversaw the horse-breeding operation. Before long, JBS began acquiring other Thoroughbreds for steeplechasing, and his horses were strong contenders or winners for some 10 years from the latter 1920s well into the 1930s.

"To supervise the social activities, Sir John turned to a young Frenchwoman, Jeanne Grenier," Vernon Snow continued. "No one knows when or how she became part of his life, but it is clear that she managed the household of Highfield.... He allowed her to name his race horses, hence their French

This is an aerial view of Highfield Stud Farm, JBS' country home near Hertford, England. A handwritten note from JBS on the back of this photo reads "Happy Yuletide, 1931, to all the Speidels. Here's hoping you have good health all of you all the year.... This is an airplane view of our little stud farm. All we need to complete the picture is your presence on a horse. May it be soon."

COURTESY JOHN BEN SNOW FOUNDATION

names of Delaneige, Delarue, and Delapaix, [and others], and he took her to the races. He provided her with a powder blue Lincoln Continental, which she used for shopping in Hoddesdon, and prior to his departure from England JBS gave Mlle. Grenier a block of securities. One wonders whether he loved her or ever proposed marriage. She remained unmarried and died in France in December 1972 shortly before the death of JBS."

In the Snow biography, Jeffrey Head, son of JBS' groom, Maurice Head, recalls JBS' favorite polo horse as "an old horse of 13-16 years called Crinkle, so called because he had

a bent ear. At the end of the game I used to take Crinkle and the other horses for a gentle cooling walk to Jepps farm and back.... During the evening a party would be held on the lawns and tennis court of the bungalow, and many is the time I used to creep back and watch through the paling fence the scene of champagne corks popping and waiters dressed as cowboys serving guests."

Merritt Speidel visited JBS in England in 1919 and the two had a fine time riding through the countryside and touring the area by car. Speidel was expanding his interests in the American newspaper business at the

Trainer Harry Beeby and JBS are shown with J. Maloney mounted on Delaneige in 1934. The horse was one of JBS' favorites.
COURTESY JOHN BEN SNOW FOUNDATION

JBS, second from right, was playing in a 1936 polo match at Highfield Stud Farm.
COURTESY JOHN BEN SNOW FOUNDATION

The two lives of John Ben Snow — horseback and suitably dressed at a foxhunt in England in the 1930s, and horseback on the Flying Horse Ranch in 1958.

COURTESY JOHN BEN SNOW FOUNDATION

time, and JBS was expanding his investment in Speidel's growing business. It was in 1936, when JBS was ready to retire and return to the United States—and when Paul Albert had just launched *The Western Horseman*— that JBS decided to visit Speidel and contemplate where to relocate for his Golden Years. Snow had intended to return to England to wind up his affairs there when the opening salvos of World War II suddenly shifted everyone's attention to a new chapter in history. German U-boats began sinking ships bound for Great Britain, and JBS' friends advised him to stay in America, and to not return to England.

Back in the USA

JBS heeded their warning, and it was just as well. In no time Highfield was turned into a military camp, the horses were all put down and buried at the edge of the polo field, and JBS never returned to his longtime home. Throughout the tough years that followed he never lost touch with those left behind in the land of his forebears, and he kept a steady supply of "care packages" shipped overseas to help his friends endure the shortages that came with war.

And so it was that JBS came to reside in Colorado Springs—the modest-size city dubbed Little London, after its genteel founder and Anglophile Gen. William Jackson Palmer. JBS lived for a time in the fabled Antlers Hotel at the west end of Pikes Peak Avenue, and eventually in an apartment across the street from the staid El Paso Club, a former mansion converted to a men's club for Colorado Springs' business elite. JBS became a member of the club and contributed English artwork to the club's décor. He maintained a suite of offices on the fourth floor of the nearby Mining Exchange Building, at Pikes Peak and Nevada Avenues.

JBS had gradually and quietly become the financier for Speidel Newspapers, and served as chairman of the board while his friend Merritt Speidel served as president. The Speidel headquarters were moved from Palo Alto, Calif., to Colorado Springs in the Mining Exchange Building, because of that central location in the country and out of respect for JBS. When JBS brought *The Western Horseman* to town, he arranged for a temporary office for the magazine in the Chamber of Commerce building. At this time he also made arrangements for construction of the unique office building for *The Western Horseman*.

The Formative Years

After Don Flint was given charge to oversee the magazine's management, one of the first things he did was look up Bob Denhardt and offer him the job of editor. Don was involved with the American Quarter Horse Association and was well aware of Bob's role in the formation of AQHA and of his early years writing for *The Western Horseman*. Bob accepted the job, beginning with the September-October 1947 issue, and proved to be well-suited for the task at hand. His wife,

Don Flint (center) in his office at The Western Horseman *met with some of the staff—from left, Marge Fernimen, Clarence Colbert, Hyde Merritt and Bob Denhardt.*

WESTERN HORSEMAN ARCHIVES

Once the latest issue was printed and shipped to the WH office, most of the staff pitched in to get the magazines in the mail to subscribers.

Sarah, and their two children moved to Reno with the understanding another move would soon be made to Colorado Springs.

Don had a nearly new staff in place when the move came in 1948. Clarence Colbert agreed to relocate from the Reno office to the Springs and oversee the circulation department. Among the new employees was a young man, Rod Koht, who went to work as bookkeeper and continued to work for the magazine for more than 30 years, becoming, along the way, circulation manager and, later, general manager and president of Western Horseman Inc. Don hired Marge Fernimen, an experienced ad person, from the *Denver Record Stockman,* and made her advertising manager for the magazine.

A cowboy friend from nearby Monument, Howard Barber, was brought in to help with mailing and distribution of the magazine, and a receptionist, Irene Rayford, was also among the new hires. Howard and Irene, who

were relatively young when hired, continued to work for the magazine until they retired; Howard spent most of his career in charge of subscription fulfillment, and Irene was promoted to the advertising department.

Rod Koht recalled those early years when the office relocated and he started to work pricing the subscription list and spreading the mail subscription liability. "At the time," Rod said, "*WH* [the initials *WH* have often been used by *Western Horseman* employees through the years, in referring to their magazine] had 12 employees and plans for an assistant editor and an advertising salesman. The budget for 1949 was payroll expense of $50,000 and all other expenses at $199,000— including printing!

"When *WH* moved to Colorado from Reno," Rod continued, "John Ben Snow owned all of *WH*, and at that time he owned most of Speidel News, too. But on July 1, 1949, there was a corporate reorganization;

Western Horseman became two separate corporations, and remained that way for several years thereafter. WH Nevada sold everything to WH Colorado, except the new office building at 3850 N. Nevada Ave., and the Nevada corporation paid the Colorado corporation for servicing the subscription list. That was how *WH* magazine went on an accrual basis for taxes, and got to write off the expense of servicing old subscribers. This is also where the mail subscription liability spread I worked on was used."

The day before this reorganization, a path was laid toward an employee-owned corporation with a Western Horseman Incorporated stock plan. On June 30, 1949, according to Rod's research, JBS had 2,496 shares of Western Horseman Colorado stock. Merritt C. Speidel, Don B. Flint, Charles H. Stout,

and Harry S. Bunker (Stout and Bunker were both JBS friends and associates from Speidel) each had 1 share—for a total of 2,500 shares. The stock ownership plan, coupled with a future employee profit-sharing arrangement, made *Western Horseman* a very desirable place to work in more ways than one. While the stock was initially held by only a handful of key employees, in time it was shared with nearly everyone who worked for the magazine, thanks to a timely stock split and increased profitability as the magazine grew in size and scope.

Staying on Target

Bob Denhardt proved to be an excellent editor for the times. He helped solidify Paul Albert's aim for the magazine to be for admirers of the western horse—interpreted

Bob Denhardt and Hyde Merritt are railbirds at the WH stable. According to a "stable log" of visitors, the earliest guests were Coke Roberds of Hayden, Colo., with two unnamed colts in October 1949, and Spike Van Cleve of Melville, Mont., with a horse named Red Man in December 1949.

WESTERN HORSEMAN ARCHIVES

This early aerial shot of the North Nevada location in Colorado Springs hung in the hallway for many years. Visitors always were amazed to see the photo of the office and stable since the city eventually grew to surround what had been a rural location.

WESTERN HORSEMAN ARCHIVES

as being either for all horses west of the Mississippi or for all horse breeds developed west of the Mississippi. "I liked the last idea," he wrote, "but who could leave out stories about Morgans, Arabs and Thoroughbreds, especially as they related to the western horse of the time?" Such stories weren't left out, and were included for many years.

Bob also realized that as the circulation continued to grow, as the number of pages in each issue increased and the deadline for articles was pushed back earlier and earlier, standard event reporting on such things as horse shows and rodeos was old news before it got to the readers. So Bob eliminated that type of reporting except for a few major events, and instead concentrated on feature articles

about top horse trainers, rodeo champions and outstanding horses.

Some readers still wanted hard news coverage of horse shows and rodeos, however, so Bob and Don put their heads together and decided to try issuing a biweekly newspaper to handle this type of reporting. It so happened that a cowboy-journalist, who had been born and raised in Wyoming and Montana, Chuck King, owned a publication titled *Bi-Weekly Rodeo News*. Chuck, unbeknownst to anyone then, was a future editor of *The Western Horseman* and he was willing to sell his rodeo newspaper to *WH* as the nucleus for its new publication, which came to be titled *The Quarter Horse News*. Hyde Merritt, a talented young cowboy and roper from Federal, Wyo., was hired to help ramrod this project, and proved to be a good fit for the job. Hyde was the son of steer roping champ King Merritt, who ranched northwest of Cheyenne, and Hyde had inherited his dad's love for good horses and good competitions.

Unfortunately, the circulation and advertising for *The Quarter Horse News* never paid for the cost of printing, and so it was dropped. Bob gave a complete collection of the publication to the AQHA for their archives. Years later, another publication (unrelated to *The Western Horseman*) was started and named *Quarter Horse News*. Ironically, this publication was acquired by what was to be *Western Horseman's* parent company years later, and is still going strong. Also of passing interest, Bob Denhardt ran across a publication that had been started in 1877 and named *The Western Horseman*. This was a bi-weekly trotting-horse paper based in Indianapolis, Indiana. After a number of years, it became *The Horseman and Fair World*.

During his tenure, Bob searched out writers and artists who had national and international reputations, with the idea this would help attract even more readers and advertisers to the magazine. He published horse-related articles by J. Frank Dobie, Joe de Yong, Luis B. Ortega and others; and ran illustrations by the likes of John Mariani, Orren Mixer, Tom Lea, George Phippen and Randy Steffen, who had designed the magazine's new office building. Don's wife, Florence, oversaw a children's feature called "Junior Horseman," and it also became a popular column. Another popular regular feature was the cartoon series written and penned by Dick Spencer III. Bob noticed how Dick "could see the strength and weaknesses of the western horseman and poke fun at him in an affectionate way."

Becoming a Monthly

While Bob was editor, he saw other major changes to the magazine—the size went from 7 x 10 inches to 8¼ x 11¼ inches (beginning in August 1948), then backed down to a slightly more economical 8 x 11 cut. *The Western Horseman* also became a monthly magazine beginning with the January 1949 issue. By year's end, circulation had reached a new high of 61,165 subscribers, including newsstand buyers.

The new monthly schedule also doubled Bob's workload, "and when combined with the necessary public relations work, put quite a strain on my time," he wrote. "I loved every minute of the work with *The Western Horseman*. However, we were now running twice as many issues each year, and twice as many pages each month. I came down with a duodenal ulcer. Because of the ulcer and the heavy workload, I decided I could no longer handle the pressures of the job."

Don asked Bob if he had a recommendation for someone to take over as editor, and Bob said yes. "I told him I knew a gifted young man who had worked for *Look* magazine, and who was not only a writer, but a cartoonist and a good horseman," Bob recalled. "At the time, he was publications editor for the University of Colorado at Boulder. Don said to call him. I did. And Dick Spencer became the fifth editor of *The Western Horseman* magazine."

He also became a legend of sorts.

3

DICK SPENCER

He WAS The Western Horseman

Don Flint and Harry Bunker made arrangements to meet Dick and his wife, JoAnne, for a job interview at Denver's Brown Palace Hotel, which was roughly halfway between Colorado Springs and Boulder, where the couple lived. Dick and Jo (everyone calls her Jo) had recently purchased a house in that town, and Jo remembers (1) she was "very pregnant" with their second daughter, Debra, at the time, and (2) that the interview for the editor's job went very well. Still, by the end of the meeting, there seemed to be something else on Don's mind as he looked at the slim, fair-skinned Dick Spencer III, who had a boyish grin and full head of hair, all of which seemed to hide his recent past as a battle-hardened World War II veteran. Don eyed him in silence for a moment. "I've got just one more question," Don said, finally.

"Yes sir," Dick said. "I'm 30 years old."

Don smiled, obviously relieved. "That's all I wanted to know." Both Dick and Jo looked younger than their years, and at that time Don wondered if the man who would be editor was really old enough to vote.

Run It Without Me

Dick Spencer's full-time career at the magazine began with the September 1951 issue. He started work in Colorado Springs that July and left Jo in Boulder to get the house sold, which she did within a month. In the interim, Dick camped in *The Western Horseman* office building; he pulled a cot out of the ladies restroom into the hallway to sleep at night.

Don told Dick, early on, that he wanted the magazine "to run without me." And Dick eagerly assumed the responsibility. As the years unfolded, Dick became synonymous with *WH*. He did what the readers did—went on trail rides and round-ups, packed into wilderness using horses and mules, helped at brandings, raised and trained horses, even bought first one ranch, then another, and lost money on cattle (like so many others). He was also a popular master of ceremonies around campfires at night, a great storyteller and entertainer when it came to telling jokes. He was an avid history buff, soaking up anything to do with cowboys, Indians, mountain men, horses and ranching. He filled the magazine with all the things he enjoyed and was interested

A youthful-appearing Dick Spencer III, during his earliest days at the magazine, is alongside Clarence Colbert, who relocated to Colorado Springs to oversee first the circulation department and later advertising for The Western Horseman.

John Ben Snow and Dick Spencer appear to be talking business in this 1953 photo taken at the Broadmoor Hotel in Colorado Springs. The scene followed the annual banquet that JBS hosted for Speidel officials from publications across the country.
COURTESY SPENCER FAMILY

in, and the readers identified with him, lived vicariously though his articles and looked forward to every issue, whether purchased off the newsstand or from the counter in the local feed-and-tack or western wear store— or taken from the mailbox each and every month, thanks to a paid-up subscription that often got renewed by a loved one every year at Christmas. When it came to putting out the magazine, Dick could do it all in the editorial department—writing, editing, cartooning, photography, page layout... and he made it look pretty easy.

Dick's Background

Dick was born January 28, 1921, to C.R. (Clifford Raymond) and Jessie Spencer, in Dallas, Texas. Dick had a brother, Bill, born a few years after he, and the two grew up together playing "cowboys and Indians." Dick became a man of many interests and talents—cartoonist, combat paratrooper

during World War II, journalist and historian, jokester, master-of-ceremonies and, of course, a horseman and successful magazine editor and publisher.

His father was also a man of varied accomplishments. He was art editor of *Collier's* and *Field & Stream* magazines, wrote instructional manuals for Army and Navy pilots under the pen name Ace McCoy, and even tried his hand at barnstorming with his own airplane. C.R. never cared for his given name and decided to change it to Richard, after his father. Thus, C.R.'s oldest son became Dick Spencer III, to eliminate confusion. And still later, Richard II became intensely interested in the history and culture of American Indians, adopted the Indian name Shatka Bear-Step, and became a masterful silversmith, making Indian jewelry and trophy belt buckles.

Dick was 7 years old and Bill was 4 when their mother suddenly abandoned them and

A photo of three generations of Spencers was used in the September 1989 issue, a tribute to Dick. From left: C.R. Spencer, who later changed his name to Richard Spencer II, and still later adopted the Indian name of Shatka Bear-Step; Richard Spencer III; and R.E. Spencer.

COURTESY SPENCER FAMILY

moved to Europe. The family was living in New York City at the time, while C.R. was working for the magazines. The boys didn't see their mother again until they were grown. At the time of abandonment, however, C.R. thought it best to take his sons to live with his father and stepmother, R.E. and Nettie Spencer, in Des Moines, Iowa. Two years later the boys rejoined their father in the Lake Worth area of Texas, and it was there the youngsters lived real-life adventures, living in a semirenovated chicken coop, roaming the woods and hunting small game with guns and live ammunition, and attending a country school in a clearing in the woods. It was also during this time that Dick developed an interest in horses, riding, cowboys, ranches and rodeo.

Attracting Attention

Throughout his life, Dick had a penchant for attracting attention. An early example: En route to school one day, Dick saw a nonpoisonous snake in the wooded path he was traveling. He did what comes natural to a lot of boys—made a lunge for the snake and caught it behind the head, thinking the reptile would make a dandy pet. That he had to put in a full day at school before he could cage the snake at home made little difference; Dick stuffed the creature into his lunch sack and continued on to school.

At the beginning of class, Dick placed his lunch at the edge of his desk, as did all the other students in class. The teacher was beginning the day's lesson when Dick's sack began to shake and crinkle. All eyes were riveted on the sack when the snake suddenly got the top untwisted and sprang straight up in the air. Pandemonium ensued, even though Dick recaptured the snake and dropped it out an open window. One student was bitten during the melee, however, and Dick earned a two-week "sabbatical." His dad never learned of the incident—Dick departed for school each morning, only to spend the day prowling the woods.

R.E. and Nettie grew increasingly concerned about Dick and Bill. They knew C.R. was away from home a lot, covering the country by motorcycle to book barnstorming shows with his airplane. They arrived at the Spencer home at Lake Worth, surveyed that situation, and simply gathered up the boys then drove back home to Des Moines. Dick and Bill had picked up Texas drawls, which sounded a little foreign to the Iowa Spencers, so arrangements were made to enroll the boys in a remedial speech class. It was a class Dick thoroughly enjoyed, because the speech therapist taught a variety of dialects (in addition to Midwestern speech), and these included British, Irish, Scottish and German. These dialects, in latter years, enhanced Dick's stories and jokes, which made him a popular campfire entertainer for groups large and small.

"Spence" on Campus

Dick met his future wife, 16-year-old JoAnne Nicholson, at a Methodist youth organization in Des Moines. The year was 1937, and such groups provided a lot of social activities for young people in the Great Depression. "We'd go roller skating, ice skating, swimming, and he was in the Methodist Boy Scout troop, too," Jo recalled. During his high school years, Dick also learned the fundamentals of horsemanship and polo by joining the Civilian Military Training Corps in Iowa.

"Spence (the name Jo and others often used for Dick in those days) was a half-year ahead of me in school, at Theodore Roosevelt High," Jo continued. "He was supposed to graduate with the January '39 class, but got sick with staphylococcus pneumonia the fall of '38 and nearly died. He had gone from 155 pounds down to 82 by the time he got out of the hospital. I was just a friend then, but

During halftime ceremonies at a 1959 University of Iowa football game, Dick was honored for creating Herky the Hawk 10 years earlier.
COURTESY SPENCER FAMILY

wrote to him every day. Anyway, he needed time to get his strength back, and put on some weight, so he wound up falling back in school and graduating with my class the following June. We dated that summer and I went to Iowa State University. He enrolled at the University of Iowa, where he also signed up with the school's ROTC (Reserve Officers' Training Corps) program.

"We didn't see each other very often," Jo said. "Summers, he always found a job somewhere, preferably at a camp as a horse wrangler. But he did other things, too. He once ran a canoe rental place on the Iowa River, worked as a lifeguard at a gravel-pit swimming hole in Des Moines; even worked in a hospital lab section feeding the experimental rats. He was always working and worked his way through college. But we dated for four years, and each time I'd get enough money together to go to Iowa City, or when he found time to hitchhike the other way, we would get together."

In college, Dick worked for board at the student union, and was paid to paint backdrops for the bands that toured college campuses for big dances in those years. He and a roommate, who had worked for a florist, even went into the corsage business, selling cut-rate corsages for guys to give to their dates when they picked them up for the dances. This enterprise involved gleaning flowers from a local cemetery, and the business literally fell apart during one of the dances. Dick and his roommate had failed to find any fresh flowers at the cemetery, so they settled for the freshest old flowers available. Before the

dance was an hour old, the floor was covered with flower petals from deteriorating corsages.

In those days, Dick also participated in a few rodeos, riding bareback broncs and bulls for "mount money," and working as a clown-bullfighter. He even found time to compete in college wrestling and diving, and was a cheerleader. He was art director for *Frivol*, the school's humor magazine, and worked part-time for the *Daily Iowan*. He began college as an art major, then switched to journalism. That combination—art and journalism— would serve him well for the rest of his life.

Combat

World War II for the United States had begun December 7, 1941, and in the fall of 1942, Dick's ROTC class was told they would be sworn into active service around Christmas that year. Dick and Jo became engaged on Christmas Eve, and Dick left the next day for Fort Benning, Ga., and Officer Candidate School. Dick and Jo were subsequently married in July 1943, right after 2nd Lt. Dick Spencer and his troops had completed parachute jump training at Camp Toccoa, across the Chattahoochee River on Fort Benning's Alabama side.

Lt. Dick Spencer III in his combat gear was ready for World War II.
COURTESY SPENCER FAMILY

Jo, meanwhile, had secured a small apartment at the main base area, on the Georgia side of the river. Dick, always a problem-solver and a strong swimmer, too, made unauthorized arrangements to visit his bride at night. He would "borrow" a jeep from the Alabama side, drive to the river, park that jeep and swim the river, holding his clothes with one hand above his head. A sergeant had a jeep waiting for him on the Georgia side, and it was easy to get dressed and drive to the apartment, where the newlyweds would have four hours together. Dick would then reverse course, swim the river back to Alabama, and be in his barracks bunk before the sound of reveille.

"We had till May 6, 1944, to be together," Jo remembered. "That's when Dick shipped out of Newport News, Va., with his company and battalion. We personally knew so many of the guys and their wives; they had been together through jump school and training at Fort Bragg, when we lived in North Carolina,

and it proved to be tough on Dick to give orders to men on dangerous patrols behind enemy lines, knowing which ones had wives back home, and which wives were pregnant. Most of his original guys didn't make it back."

Dick was a prolific letter-writer to Jo, and did his writing on a portable typewriter he managed to keep throughout the war. The typewriter was given to him in 1939 by his grandparents. Dick kept a log for his outfit, the 517 Parachute Combat Team, and later became a correspondent for *Stars and Stripes,* writing about the 517th's exploits; after the war, he published a booklet on the 517th for all the men who served in the outfit.

It was on the Italy-France invasion one day that a bomb hit the jeep Dick was riding in, killing the driver. "Spence said he was riding along and a small, still voice told him to put on his helmet, which he did," Jo recalled. "He was wounded, but that helmet saved his life — and the typewriter survived as well."

Right after the war, Dick wrote and illustrated this booklet on his 517 Parachute Combat Team.
COURTESY SPENCER FAMILY

He was wounded two other times. He took grenade fragments in his face, and a sniper shot him in the buttocks. Dick would come home a captain, following Germany's surrender, having earned the Silver Star and a Purple Heart with two oak clusters. In all, he made 22 fighting jumps in the invasions of Italy, France, Belgium and Germany.

Dick related some of his war experiences, often over coffee breaks at *The Western Horseman* office. The stories weren't filled with gory details or heroics, but usually involved a bit of humor or irony. He told of the troops, during the battle in Italy, fighting through olive groves while suffering from severe dysentery. "It got so bad," Dick recalled, "that men had to cut out the seats of their pants. There wasn't a clean pair of underwear in the whole battalion."

When Dick's jeep blew up, he was incapacitated with injuries. Fellow soldiers hid him in a straw-manure pile inside a stable, while the fighting raged on around them. The men fashioned an air hole for Dick using a jacket sleeve that protruded inconspicuously out of the pile. That afternoon, Dick heard troops from both sides coming and going through the stable. Then there was quiet. One of the guys who helped hide him, an old college pal named Pinkston, walked up to the straw pile and shouted down the sleeve: "Spence! Are ya still there?"

Dick was sent to a recovery unit near Nice. His arm had been injured and was swollen with tetanus from the manure when he arrived. A doctor asked where he had been. "I've been in a lot of deep crap," Dick replied. He recovered and made it back to his outfit in time for a railroad trip to the Battle of the Bulge. "They put us on some old box cars called 40-and-8s, built for World War I to haul 40 men and 8 horses," Dick said. "And I don't think the straw had been changed in those cars since World War I." The men were quickly covered with tortuous little parasites called scabies, which were in the straw. That itching was terrible, and to get rid of them the men eventually stripped, doused themselves with sulfa powder, and were given new clothing. "We all stood on the ground on sections of newspaper, and when that powder came, you could hear those little buggers when they fell off and hit the paper," Dick said. His feet froze during the Battle of the Bulge, but at least he didn't lose any toes.

After the War

Dick's outfit returned home in September 1945. The men took a train from Boston to Chicago where they were to officially muster out of the service. As soon as the train slowed, going through the Chicago rail yards, most of the men simply jumped off. They were close to home and didn't want to go through any formalities. Dick and Jo had a daughter by then, Bobbi Jo (whom Dick had not yet seen), and Mom and daughter were living in Des Moines. Bobbi Jo stayed with

● "Whoa, steady boy—easy does it . . ."   ● "Simmer down now, ya ornery critter! Quit sucking in wind — yer being saddled by an old cowhand!"   ● "Hey Pop! I did it all by myself! N[o] will ya get me a real pony?"

This cartoon strip, titled "Bucky" for the little kid in the ongoing series, was among Dick Spencer's earliest work in the magazine. This particular cartoon appeared in the January 1949 issue.

WESTERN HORSEMAN ARCHIVES

Here's Dick in the "wild cow riding" on Santa Catalina Island in 1964.
LES WALSH PHOTO/*WESTERN HORSEMAN* ARCHIVES

family while Jo took a train to Chicago to meet her husband.

They returned to Des Moines and Dick got a job with Steinel Publications, which produced several law enforcement periodicals. Then he landed a job with *Look* magazine, starting at $35 a week in salary and later increasing to $55. The Spencers were working their way up. They built a small house in town in 1947 and the following year their son, Rick, was born, and Dick took a job at his alma mater, the University of Iowa.

He taught magazine production plus a new class, editorial cartooning. He had some great students, including Paul Conrad, who went on to win a Pulitzer Prize for editorial cartooning. During the nearly three years Dick was at the university he wrote a couple of books—*Pulitzer Prize Cartoons* and *Editorial Cartooning, the Techniques and Tricks of the Trade.* Dick also created the school's mascot—Herky the Hawk—which is still in

use today. Dick enjoyed his post-war stint in college; he even served as head cheerleader and was voted Big Man on Campus, a real honor in those days. The move to Boulder came next, and then employment with *The Western Horseman.* Thirty days after Dick started work at the magazine, he and Jo, and children Barbara Jo (Bobbi Jo), Richard Craig (Rick), and soon to be followed by youngest daughter Debra Jean (Debbie), moved to a house on a hill less than two miles from the office building.

The house, Dick recalled, was perfect for the family, and they knew it as soon as they saw it. They built a stable out back, overlooking several large valleys filled with interesting rock formations and pine trees. For years, the Spencers had permission to pasture horses in those valleys; they rode in them, the kids camped out in caves located on some of the rock ledges, and the scenic area often served as photo backdrops for pictures that

Rodeo clowns deluxe—Dick and John Harris volunteered to be the clown-bullfighters at the Little Britches Rodeo in Breckenridge one year.
COURTESY SPENCER FAMILY

appeared in the magazine. Dick often rode a horse to work—the area was still pretty rural—and he usually kept one he was training at the office stable. He was editor of the "World's Leading Horse Magazine" (as each magazine cover proclaimed) and he was living the life he loved. His first horse, an Appaloosa mare, was given the Indian name He Topa. In those days, owners and breeders often gave their Appaloosas Indian names. Bobbi Jo remembers how, after supper, her dad would put the mare on a long lead line in the back yard, smoke his pipe and just watch her graze. As did many of the magazine's readers, Dick Spencer simply enjoyed watching his horse in the evening.

This shot is of a more mature Dick Spencer and the smile many remember so well.

The
WESTERN
HORSEMAN

JANUARY 1955 • 35 CENTS

TWENTIETH YEAR of the WESTERN HORSEMAN

The Magazine for Admirers of Stock Horses

• **RANCHERS**   • **CONTESTANTS**   • **BREEDERS**   • **RIDING CLUBS**

4

THE 1950S

Growth and Prosperity

The 1950s were great for the Spencers and great for the magazine—a decade of growth and prosperity. Television became common in homes, and westerns were among the most popular programs on television and at the movies—youngsters wanted to ride horses and ponies. In 1951, the same year Dick was hired, *The Western Horseman* expanded its newsstand presence by joining with International Circulation Distributors, a magazine distributor based in New York City. Such companies, then and now, work with regional magazine wholesalers to help get magazines on newsstands. The *WH* and ICD relationship would last for the next 50 years and beyond, and *WH* circulation would climb as the magazine was introduced to many new readers each month via newsstands throughout the continent.

The Flying Horse Ranch

In 1953, Don Flint's title went from general manager to publisher. The popular annual all-breed issue, devoted to updating readers on activities inside the various horse registries, began in 1956, and a Texan named Ray Davis was hired as breeders' service representative in 1958. Ray went on to become a field

editor and popular editorial contributor with his monthly column "Headin' an' Heelin'."

Don Flint still tried to keep the office at arm's length, but he often would stop by on his way into town from the Flying Horse Ranch. Ralph Lavelett, who headed up the *WH* mailroom, remembers how Don would park his car by the back door and leave the vehicle running, because he planned to be inside for only a minute. Don would get tied up more often than not and Ralph was accustomed to the sound of the car engine running outside. After 30 minutes, Ralph would go outside and turn off the key. Don also was accustomed to relying on men in the *WH* office for any day labor needed on the ranch. Working on a branding crew was part of being a *WH* staffer for some of the men. Ralph remembers the time he and Howard Barber were even recruited to haul some of the ranch horses to California.

For the record—the Flying Horse Ranch was financed by JBS, but Don and Florence Flint held title to the property. That was the arrangement JBS wanted, and the property included a beautiful home that JBS named Highfield West, because it reminded him of the estate he left behind in England. "There

The January 1955 cover featured horses and riders outside the WH *building, and announced the "Twentieth Year of* The Western Horseman. *"*

Weather was cool and grass was dormant when this scene was photographed on the Flying Horse Ranch in the 1950s. Mount Herman, part of Colorado's Front Range, rises in the background. Today, this area is filled with homes, paved streets and golf courses.

COURTESY SPENCER FAMILY

Ray Davis became another long-time WH staffer after signing on with the outfit in 1958. He lived and traveled extensively in Texas, reporting on rodeos, ropings, and ranches.

Here's a pasture full of fillies on the Flying Horse Ranch in the 1950s. Don Flint was a regular Quarter Horse advertiser in WH at this time. A knowledgeable horseman, he stayed very much abreast of developments in the breed, and contributed a few feature stories and editorials on the subject.

was an English dining room with murals depicting a fox hunt and a fireplace framed by wood paneling, a French kitchen with an open hearth fireplace and beamed ceilings, a breakfast alcove furnished in Georgian décor, a large wine room with a corner bar and indoor shuffleboard court, a recreation room with a piano and a billiard table, a large American-style living room (called the main lounge) with an Oriental corner, and, of course, a trophy room filled with mementos and photographs portraying polo matches, fox hunts, and races of years gone by," wrote Vernon Snow.

John Ben Snow, meanwhile, had settled into a routine involving almost daily horseback rides at the Flying Horse Ranch. Mornings, he would drive his Rolls Royce convertible from the Antlers Hotel Garage and head north on Nevada Ave., past the *WH* office. He rarely stopped at the office, but would attend the annual *WH* stockholders meeting. One day, however, he did stop abruptly, walked into the office and demanded to know why the flag wasn't flying atop the pole out front. From that point on, it was a rare occasion when Old Glory wasn't raised in the morning and retired at the end of each workday. Following his morning ride, JBS would drive back to town and spend the rest of the day in his office, which adjoined the Speidel offices at the top of the Mining Exchange Building.

Dick and Appaloosas

During this time, Dick was still enamored with Appaloosa horses, and he and George Hatley, a founder of the Appaloosa Horse Club at Moscow, Idaho, became good friends. Dick bought and sold Appaloosas, wrote about them in the magazine and in the process gave this Nez Perce Indian breed a tremendous boost. People across the country created a demand for this colorful breed, thanks largely to the publicity Dick gave those horses in the magazine. Dick and the family participated in trail rides and horse shows around the country. Bobbi Jo remembers an Appaloosa show she and her dad went to at Estes Park, Colorado. Dick rented

The Spencer kids in 1958— Bobbi Jo, Rick and Debbie—as they appeared on the family Christmas card.
COURTESY SPENCER FAMILY

Merry Christmas
THE SPENCERS

Dick was 35 years old when he posed for this 1956 picture with one of his first Appaloosas, He Topa.

COURTESY SPENCER FAMILY

The Western Horseman Book Line

Toward the end of the 1950s, Dick introduced a line of books published by *The Western Horseman* as a service to readers. This also would be a service to the staff, who continuously answered questions by phone or letter concerning the basics of owning, riding and caring for horses. The staff could simply recommend the appropriate book. The horse industry was thriving at the time, but there was relatively little in the way of books published along the lines of equine health care, training and other related topics. *Beginning Western Horsemanship*, by Editor Dick Spencer III, had 32 pages of articles that included the basics of riding and caring for horses. The booklet made its debut in 1959, after having run as a series of articles in the magazine, and sold for $1. Bobbi Jo was pictured with a horse on the cover.

By 1960, *The Western Horseman* had a circulation of 117,853. A one-year subscription cost $4 and the single-copy price was 50 cents. The office hours had been adjusted to 7:45 a.m. to 4:15 p.m., with 30 minutes for lunch. This schedule best fit around the heavy construction traffic traveling to and fro past the office each day while work progressed on the United States Air Force Academy, farther north and directly west of the Flying

a stall at the fairgrounds for their horse, Wasi Massa, plus a stall for the two of them to sleep in, using sleeping bags on hay. The show featured a costume class in which participants dressed in carefully researched Indian regalia, and the winner was determined by audience applause. Bobbi Jo was in the audience, waiting for the class to begin, when a man walked by offering nickels to children who agreed to clap for his wife, who was riding in the class. "I'm sorry," Bobbi Jo told the man. "I can't take your money because my dad is riding in that class." Dick finished second that day.

"Every trip we took as a family, Dad always carried his camera and always stopped at historical markers," Bobbi Jo said. "He'd interview people along the way; for example, we went on the Chief Joseph Trail Ride and he stopped by the Crow Indian Agency to visit and learn. He'd get several stories out of each trip, and we'd see them show up later in the magazine."

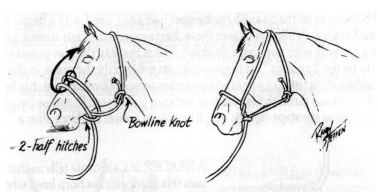

THIS ROPE HALTER is easy to tie whenever you need to lead a horse and you don't have a ready-made halter at hand. First, tie a bowline to form a fairly snug loop around the neck, up close to the throat. Then, using the free end, throw two half-hitches around the nose; take the loop of the hitch closest to the horse's eyes, pull it toward the nose and under the second half-hitch, and then place it over the poll, back of the ears. Work the rope around until it fits well, and lead him off. It won't tighten down when tied right, and will be comfortable to your horse.

Randy Steffen's art and helpful ideas, which appeared regularly in the magazine, were compiled in the popular Horseman's Scrapbook.

Beginning Western Horsemanship, *the first in a now long line of* Western Horseman *books, featured Bobbi Jo Spencer on the cover.*

Horse Ranch. The A.B. Hirschfeld Press in Denver printed the magazine in those days, and Dick and Jo would drive up to the printer each month with the magazine "dummy"—the cut-and-paste version of the magazine that the Hirschfeld staff would use to assemble and print the magazine.

Dick and other staff members went on to introduce more new books. Topics included intermediate and advanced western horsemanship, horseshoeing and hoof care, health problems of the horse, and the popular *Horseman's Scrapbook,* by Randy Steffen, whose pen-and-ink drawings and handy hints for horsemen appeared regularly in the magazine. Dick came out with *Horse Breaking,* and explained that it was a "how-to-do-it book that tells in words and pictures the step-by-step process for breaking your own colt with a minimum of danger to both you and your horse." A lot of photos appearing in the book were taken in the corrals at the office stable.

Riding the Range

Trail riding was Dick's favorite horse activity. Riding through mountains, plains or desert, visiting with other riders along the way, was a natural pastime for him. He became a member of the local Pikes Peak Range Riders, a men's riding organization that annually rode around Pikes Peak, promoting Colorado Springs' Pikes Peak or Bust Rodeo each summer. John Ben Snow and Harry S. Bunker (Snow's right-hand man who served as secretary of Western Horseman, Inc.) also were members of the group. The ride, still going strong, begins with a public street breakfast in downtown, served by cooks from nearby Fort Carson, and then the riders head west for the five-day trek. In Dick's time with the group, they often covered 20 miles or more per day. Dick served as master of ceremonies around the campfires at night, regaling the crowd with jokes and stories. He was also a member of

Dick showed this youngster at the 1956 National Western Stock Show in Denver.

the Desert Caballeros, who made a similar annual ride out of Wickenburg, Ariz., each year. One year he went on California's grueling Tevis Cup Ride, in which participants ride 100 miles through the High Sierras in one day. Dick accepted invitations to pack into various wilderness-type areas, including Yellowstone National Park. Accounts of these various rides would invariably show up in future issues of the magazine.

Dick always carried one of the office cameras, which took good black-and-white photos, especially if they were still photos of groups, individuals, horses, scenery and so forth; the cameras used black-and-white film and required a person to look downward into a viewfinder. They preceded the 35-millimeter, single-lens-reflex cameras. Almost all the photos used in the magazine in those days were black-and-white. Always careful with a dollar, Dick headed out on a trip with one, maybe two rolls of film. He created a darkroom in a broom closet in the lower level of the office, where he and other staffers developed and printed their own pictures.

Spence's Humor

Dick found humor in most everything. The jokes he told ranged from spontaneous "one-liners" to lengthy stories involving one or more of the dialects he was so good at using. Much of his humor was slightly racy, but told in such a way that it offended no one. He used to say, somewhat laconically, "I only know one clean joke." He actually knew a lot more than that, and knew a variety of different punch lines to the same joke. People asked how he could possibly remember all those jokes. Dick would reply, "Well, for every joke I remember, I forget two names."

He was also a firm believer in the adage, "Never let the facts get in the way of a good story." It would be impossible to effectively replicate his jokes on these pages, but suffice to say they often involved a surprise ending. For example: the Irish priest who listens to Mrs. O'Malley's confession of hitting her husband over the head with an iron skillet when he came home drunk... "Well," the good Father says with a brogue, "that was a bad thing to do. Give me ten Hail Marys and

In the 1950s, John Ben Snow liked to bring Speidel publishing executives from around the country to Colorado Springs for a round of meetings and a banquet at the exclusive Broadmoor Hotel. The Speidel gatherings must have been fun, especially with Dick Spencer as resident joke-teller. This photo, taken in 1953, shows JBS, center, and other Speidel executives, possibly reacting to a punch line delivered by Dick Spencer, seated next to JBS.

COURTESY SPENCER FAMILY

During one of the annual banquets, Rod Koht, seated, visits with an unidentified Speidel executive. Standing at left are Dick Spencer and Clarence Colbert, with Don Flint at the far right.
COURTESY SPENCER FAMILY

next time he comes home drunk, use a rollin' pin instead of the skillet."

Dick had heard a simple joke about a Mexican submarine, and added it to his collection after much embellishment. The scene involved the launching of "Mexico's first submarine," as, of course, described by a "witness" using a Mexican dialect. Speeches were made, a Mariachi band performed, charros entertained the crowd with intricate rope-spinning routines, and finally it was time to launch the submarine. The vessel slid into the water and disappeared, then bubbles began to appear on the surface of the bay, followed by a tremendous bubble that brought forth a sole survivor who swam to shore and told how leaks began to appear in the hull, one after the other, "an' finally the whole adobe wall caved in!"

Dick had some close friends who were of Irish descent, Mexican and most every other nationality. Through the years, he told and swapped jokes with folks from virtually all backgrounds—anyone who appreciated a good laugh. He told the late astronaut Wally Schirra an astronaut joke, and they became friends. He once "helped" the late singer John Denver with a song-fest around a campfire. And whenever a reader came through the front door of the office, Dick would drop whatever he was doing to visit and personally conduct an office tour, if that's what the guest wanted.

Throughout his life, Dick drew cartoons both for the magazine and as impromptu cards for friends and co-workers. He took along cartooning supplies on trail rides, just to be able to present a humorous card/drawing to someone on the ride who might be celebrating a birthday or anniversary, or to brighten the day of anyone who might have had a trail mishap. Sometimes, Dick was the one who suffered the accident. He broke his ankle on one ride, far from medical help. In the spirit of the Old West, Dick shoved his foot into his boot, before the swelling started, and finished the ride, which went on for several more days.

As the years unfolded, Dick also tried a variety of other activities—he enjoyed scuba diving, flying, hunting, fishing and skiing. Typically, he would concentrate on one new activity for a spell, master it, then drop it and go on to something else. He and his family made regular weekend jaunts to Breckenridge, a ski town in the mountains west of Colorado Springs, where they bought a quaint house they called "The Chalet." And they bought their first ranch, named The Arrowhead, also in the mountains. "We bought that place from Bill and Eleanor Mueller—350 acres they sold while squaring off their ranch, which today is Mueller State Park," Jo recalled. "It had an old cabin on it, and two rentals, and Spence said if you'd flatten it out it'd be as big as Texas. We enjoyed it for several years, then found out about the Gold Pan Ranch (nearby). We got 900 acres plus some BLM land and a school section (640 acres). We got it cheap, and had fun with it. Dick didn't like maintenance, so we hired most of that done, even though we didn't have a lot of money. Every extra nickel went to buy *Western Horseman* stock as it became available." The ranches, especially the Gold Pan, were a source of magazine material for several years.

5

MORE GROWTH

Increases in Staff, Circulation, Advertising

The 1960s saw more growth in the magazine. Circulation continued to climb and more advertising came in, which resulted in more editorial pages that needed to be filled in each issue. One of the positions that needed to be filled in 1961 was that of editorial assistant, and Dick perused a letter and resumé that had been sent to the magazine office about that same time, asking about a job.

Pat Close

Patricia A. Close, an avid horsewoman, was hired by Dick as editorial assistant on September 1, 1961. Pat was born July 26, 1935, in Miami, Florida. One summer, during World War II, her dad sent her and her mother and brother to a Montana ranch owned by a longtime friend. Pat remembers how "we just rode all summer, like wild Indians, didn't know anything about horsemanship but had a wonderful time. And then when I was in junior high, my mother got me a horse and it proceeded from there." Pat was hooked on horses.

Pat competed in Florida's big winter all-breed shows in open western classes in the 1950s, and also went to the University of Florida, where she was graduated in 1957 with a degree in animal science and a minor in journalism. Shortly after graduation she moved to Urbana, Ill., to work at the University of Illinois Agricultural Extension Editorial Office, and it was during this time she purchased a registered Quarter Horse gelding and began competing in AQHA shows. But Pat never forgot the childhood rides on that Montana ranch. She still wanted to get out west, so she applied for a job at *The Western Horseman*. She remembers how Dick picked her up at one of the two train stations in town for an interview. A couple weeks later, he phoned Pat to tell her she had a job. She and her horse "and a few meager belongings" arrived in Colorado Springs over the Labor Day weekend, and she embarked on a career that would see her working for the magazine for the next 40 years, going from editorial assistant to associate editor,

Pat Close and her horse made for a great picture in front of the office building one day during the 1960s. The photo was used in the book Riding and Training for the Show Ring, *written by Pat Close and Mona Betts, a top trainer and rider whose family raised Arabians.*

Skijoring behind the office in winter of 1965, Pat Close and Chuck King were horseback, towing Chan Bergen and another staffer on skis.

WESTERN HORSEMAN ARCHIVES

Pat Close always has been a competitor. Here she is on "Chubby" at the 1969 Colorado State Fair in the senior Quarter Horse reining.

DAROL DICKINSON

managing editor, and finally, editor and vice-president of Western Horseman Inc.

Pat bought an acreage north of town in the Black Forest, an easy drive to the office; her life revolved around horses, dogs and the magazine. One of her best horses, in later years, was Skipit Chex, a mare by the renowned King Fritz. Professional trainer Al Dunning successfully showed "Checkers" for Pat in the hackamore in several major West Coast open American Horse Shows Association events. And Checkers eventually raised several nice foals for Pat.

Pat bought an Arabian gelding, Lisaam ("Sam") in 1971 that she showed on the local, regional, and national level, and later added a couple Quarter Horse geldings to her family—Reggie and Harley—that she used for ranch work and trail riding. Dick always encouraged *Western Horseman* staffers, particularly those who worked in the editorial department, to be active in the horse industry, and Pat took that encouragement to heart. In the 1960s she volunteered as an instructor for local 4-H horse clubs, and helped organize the El Paso County Horsemen's Council. While serving on this council she worked to protect horse owners from proposed zoning ordinances aimed at eliminating horses in backyards or on small acreages. And she also

And here's Pat in 1977 on Lisaam ("Sam") at the U.S. National Championship Arabian Horse Show, where Sam was the reserve national champion trail horse.
COURTESY PAT CLOSE

promoted the development or expansion of local equine facilities used by the public.

For the magazine, Pat was the go-to person when it came to horse-show competition, questions about bloodlines, top trainers, equine health care… and spelling and punctuation. As years went by, she became a major contributor to the *WH* book department, conceiving ideas, writing the copy, and seeing the various book projects through production.

Chuck King

A meaningful life for Charles G. King came down to three things: being a cowboy, being a good roper, and working for *The Western Horseman.* The first two he accomplished in timely fashion growing up in Wyoming and Montana, where his father worked as a game warden. The last one took a little longer, but he got there. Chuck was born December 23, 1918, in Clark, Wyo., and was graduated from high school in Cody in 1936, after having lettered in football and basketball. The following year found him studying magazine illustration, layout and design at the Chicago Academy of Art. This was followed by a year at the Corcoran Art School in Washington, D.C.

As with so many other men of his generation, he wound up serving his country in World War II—in the Army Air Corps with the Flying Tigers, and during that time he worked his way up to the rank of sergeant. Chuck never talked much about the war—to him it was something he had to do and he did it. But he did learn photography in the Air Corps, and perhaps the brightest spot in the whole war, for Chuck, occurred overseas when he got to compete in an all-servicemen's rodeo and won the bull-riding event.

Chuck was discharged in November 1945, but instead of moving back to Wyoming, as one might have guessed, he worked a little over a year as a lithographer for the U.S. Coast and Geodetic Survey, in Washington, D.C. This was followed by a year in which he worked for *Bit and Spur* magazine, out of Billings, Montana. Then Chuck started his own publication, the *Bi-Weekly Rodeo News,* which was purchased by *WH* (as explained in Chapter Two). Chuck was managing editor

No one loved working on the WH staff more than Chuck King. He once remarked that working in the office was "sorta like being in a bunkhouse." Of course, Chuck wasn't above leaving the office a little early to go home and rope.
WESTERN HORSEMAN ARCHIVES

a regional Quarter Horse organization. His specialty at the magazine was writing about roping and rodeo, and he illustrated many of his articles with his own artwork, as well as with photos.

Chan Bergen

Chandler W. Bergen was born October 12, 1919, in Madison, New Jersey. By the time he was graduated from Madison High School he had developed a keen interest in outdoor activities—sports like skiing, hunting, fishing, hiking and climbing; anything, in fact, that promised to be adventurous. As years went by, Chan's quests for these activities were fulfilled. He kayaked across the English Channel, climbed the Matterhorn, became an excellent skier, and enjoyed fishing in mountain streams. All of this was courtesy of World War II and the United States Army.

In 1940, Chan initially had gone to work for International Business Machine Corporation on Madison Avenue in New York City. Chan liked the company but soon grew tired of an office job in the big city. He

of the publication during its brief life as *The Quarter Horse News*, under the ownership of *WH*. After that, Chuck did return to Wyoming, where he worked as a cowboy, horse-breaker and dude wrangler for a variety of ranches in the northern part of the state. The passage of time found this once foot-loose cowboy with a wife and family. Chuck and Margaret King had a son, Mac, and Chuck worked a steady job as a draftsman for the Gulf Oil Corporation in Billings. Through the years, Chuck stayed in pretty close touch with Dick Spencer, assuring Dick he was ready to take a job with *The Western Horseman* whenever the opportunity arose.

On March 18, 1963, Chuck was hired as assistant editor, and he brought with him a perspective of the horse industry from the eyes of a rodeo contestant. Chuck was an avid team roper who competed in the Rodeo Cowboys Association. He also belonged to the National Cutting Horse Association and

This is the photo Chan used in his monthly "Editorial Scene" column.
COURTESY CHAN BERGEN

Here's Chan mounted on his good horse Rev.
COURTESY CHAN BERGEN

sized up the world situation, figured he would be drafted sooner or later, and went to the nearest recruiting office to join the Army in June 1941. When the United States was officially pulled into the war six months later, Chan looked upon the situation as an epic adventure not to be missed.

On December 7, 1942—one year after the Japanese attack on Pearl Harbor—2nd Lt. Bergen sailed out of Pearl Harbor as a platoon leader with the 27th Infantry Regiment, part of the 25th Division. The entire division was on troop transports, and three weeks later landed at Guadalcanal, to relieve the 1st Marine Division, which had been in combat for more than four months, and whose ranks had been depleted with injuries, deaths and malaria.

Chan's first taste of battle involved taking a hill in the jungle, beyond the Marine perimeter, on January 10. By February 7 and 8, the island had been cleared of all resistance. Still, there were air raids, the nightly bombing of Henderson Airfield. Chan's platoon was guarding some large artillery pieces on the north coast of Guadalcanal the day he watched the major air battle over the harbor involving fighters and bombers.

Chan was overseas for three-and-a-half years and was in other major battles after Guadalcanal. There was the battle for New Georgia Island, just north of Guadalcanal in the Solomon Island group, an assault landing on another nearby island, and finally a hard-fought slog from January to mid-June 1945 in the battle for Luzon in the Philippines, up Highway 5, where Japanese artillery was stationed in jungle caves at each turn of the road. Throughout the war, Chan and his rifle platoon experienced the full range of battle—artillery and aerial bombardment, beach landings, intense jungle firefights, and debilitating sickness.

After Luzon, the division was preparing for an assault landing on the island of Honshu and the Japanese homeland when word was received that an atomic bomb had hit Hiroshima. "We had never heard of an atomic bomb until then," Chan recalled. "I was always grateful to Harry Truman, who

Chan and Rev went out for a winter's ride at the Bergen place, Rancho Robles (Ranch of the Oaks).
COURTESY CHAN BERGEN

gave the go-ahead to use that weapon. If we had made an assault landing on that island, the casualty rate would have been terrific. As it was, we landed unopposed and I wouldn't say we were welcomed, but we had no opposition, no problems."

Chan grew to love Japan and its people. He stayed the winter of 1945 and '46, working as regimental communications officer, and spent weekends skiing the Japanese slopes. In 1948 he was assigned to Germany, with the occupying army there, and fell in love with that country, too. He served with the First Division and assisted with communications efforts during the Berlin Airlift. It was also in Germany that he met his future wife, Melitta Niitsoo, a displaced person from Estonia who lost her family in the war and was working as an interpreter for the American Red Cross in Ansbach. Chan nearly lost track of Melitta when she immigrated to the United States, but found her again, this time in Denver, where she was working as a bookkeeper. They were married in 1953, shortly after he had arrived at Camp Carson near Colorado Springs, where he was assigned to Mountain and Cold Weather Training.

Melitta was the perfect mate for Chan. She was a skilled fly fisher and avid skier who had an appreciation for travel and the arts. As spouse of a military officer, Melitta traveled with Chan to duty stations again in Japan, in the United States, and again in Germany. After more than two decades in the U.S. Army, Chan retired as a lieutenant colonel in 1963, and he and Melitta settled in Colorado Springs, where she went to work in the accounting department for the local school district, and Chan did some free-lance magazine writing while looking for steady work.

"I never pretended to be a horseman, and had never heard of *The Western Horseman* magazine," Chan recalled, "I'd just finished a 21-year career in the infantry; Melitta and I were in Colorado Springs, and I was looking for a decent job. I was downtown one day in the main library and went in to browse, and saw a copy of *The Western Horseman* on the rack. I thought, 'Gee, that looks interesting.' In that issue, Dick had done a story on the Arrowhead Ranch; I read it and thought it all looked like a lot of fun."

Chan later walked into an employment office, paid 50 cents to fill out an application, and handed it to the man behind the desk, a retired Air Force colonel named Hugh Blaine. "Chan," Hugh sighed, "the town is full of guys like you—retired military. I don't have anything that would interest you...." Hugh and Chan visited a minute, then Hugh said, "Oh, there is a job, not far from here, but I'm afraid you wouldn't want it. It's at a magazine called *The Western Horseman.*"

"I darned near jumped out of the chair," Chan said, "and I was already thinking this might get my foot in the door. So I ended up with an interview with Rod Koht, who spent a lot of time with me describing this job in the circulation department."

Rod concluded the interview by asking Chan if there was anything else he wanted to know. "I don't know if I impress you, Mr. Koht, but I really want this job," Chan said. "I like everything about it."

"Don't you want to know what the job pays?" Rod smiled.

Chan hadn't even thought about it. He liked the people and the building, and just knew he wanted to work there. Rod said he had some others to interview, but would call Chan one way or the other. A week went by before Rod called. "You got the job," he said, and that's how it started for Chan, who went to work as mailroom clerk in the circulation department on January 23, 1964.

The circulation department was in the lower level of the building—a walkout basement that leads to the parking lot. Chan showed up for work wearing a blue suit and striped tie. Howard Barber, his boss, shook hands with him and said, "You don't look like you're ready to go to work—better take off that tie." *The Western Horseman*, then and now, has enjoyed a casual western-attire dress code. Chan went to work on the Address-O-Graph machine, a noisy contraption that, nonetheless, served its purpose. The machine had a keyboard that would bang out subscriber names and addresses—one letter or number at a time—on metal plates that resembled military dog tags. The plates would print address labels for manila envelopes used to mail out the magazines.

Chan had worked a good two years in circulation when he decided to ask Rod for permission to visit with Dick Spencer, to see if there might be a place for him upstairs in the editorial department. Rod said go ahead, so Chan visited with Dick and handed him some *Outdoor Life* articles he had done while in the service. Dick said he would keep that in mind, and several weeks later he called Chan upstairs to his office.

"Chan," Dick said, "I've got a job for you; you're going to be a book editor... I'll teach you everything you need to know."

Dick assigned Chan the job of creating and overseeing future books to be published as part of the expanding *WH* book collection. Dick moved another desk into his office, for Chan to work at, and helped Chan get his feet on the ground. One of the first books Chan put together was *Rodeo Pictures,* by the great rodeo photographer DeVere Helfrich. That was followed by *Games on Horseback,* which depicted a variety of fun contests involving horses. Dick showed Chan how to use one of the office cameras and develop film in the darkroom by "sloshing it around in some chemicals, rinsing it off in tap water and hanging it on an overhead wire to dry," Chan remembered.

Chan shot about a dozen rolls of film for the *Games* book, developed the film in the darkroom, and found that the film came out slightly over-developed; it was mid-summer and the chemicals and tap water were warmer than usual, thus overdeveloping the film. Chan looked into a more controlled process for developing black-and-white film, feeding a roll of film into a canister, checking the temperatures of chemicals and rinse water, and timing the process according to a film chart. Chan was justifiably proud of the outcome, which resulted in better quality photos for the magazine as well as the book department.

Push This Damn Thing

The staff continued to grow and in 1966 the office building was expanded by taking both levels farther out back. That was also the year WH Inc. Director Harry S. Bunker died. Harry's last wishes were that his ashes be taken to a favorite high-mountain trail frequented by the Pikes Peak Range Riders. Dick made all the arrangements. A group of riders would convene atop a unique outcropping of flat rocks called The Pancakes. Dick would dress up in authentic Indian regalia and preside over the little outdoor service, presenting The Lord's Prayer in Indian sign language while a musical recording of the prayer played on a small tape recorder.

Chan would accompany the group and be responsible for starting the tape player. Dick showed Chan how to operate the device the previous day at the office. "Now, you push this damn thing here and that'll get it going," Dick explained. Next day, high atop the mountain, the party dismounted and gathered for Harry's service with hats in

Harry Bunker's Ashes

This photo is of Harry S. Bunker, a director for WH Inc., on one of the Pikes Peak Range Rides.
COURTESY SPENCER FAMILY

After Harry passed away, his ashes were taken by members of the Range Riders high atop The Pancakes rock formation near Cripple Creek, Colo., to be scattered.
COURTESY SPENCER FAMILY

A prayer and kind words were said...
COURTESY SPENCER FAMILY

... and then Dick presented his version of the Lord's Prayer in Indian sign language while Chan Bergen played the recording of a musical version of the prayer. Dick made his own Indian clothing (and in a similar vein made a mountain-man outfit, too).
COURTESY SPENCER FAMILY

hand while the ashes were scattered and Dick stepped forward to begin The Lord's Prayer in sign language. He gave Chan the signal and the recording began: "Now, you push this damn thing here and that'll get it going…."

The rest of the service went off without a hitch, and Dick produced a small wooden cross he had made to mark the site. Dick never flustered easily, and as usual he figured a little humor, intended or not, never hurt. There was consternation one day in the advertising department when it was discovered an extra period had inadvertently been placed in an advertisement's stud fee for a stallion. It looked like the stud fee was $30.0.00 instead of $300.00. "Well," Dick smiled, before walking off, "it's better to have an extra period rather than miss a period altogether."

JBS—Still Riding

John Ben Snow, meanwhile, was getting older, but refused to give up riding. Friends and associates grew increasingly concerned for his safety, especially if he was riding alone, but no one was about to tell JBS his riding days were over. Dick spent time with JBS' horse in the corral behind the office, making sure the horse was "bombproof." As a test, Dick even slid off the side of the horse, intentionally falling to the ground with his foot still in the stirrup—and the horse seemed unperturbed with the situation. JBS continued to ride, but unfortunately his rides weren't around the Flying Horse Ranch after 1965. Don and Florence sold the ranch that year, and frankly, this strained their relationship with JBS, who continued his rides on a small, nearby ranch owned by Glen Scribner. JBS was 83 years old and often rode alone through Scribner's rocky hills and pine forest six days a week.

The inevitable accident came in 1966. JBS was unhorsed and taken to the hospital with extensive bruises but fortunately no broken bones. He was released a week later and resumed his routine. The following February, however, he suffered a similar riding accident, and this time, following treatment and a round of tests, the doctor told JBS what no one had wanted to tell him—his riding days were over.

Well, not entirely over. JBS located a three-speed mechanical horse, and had it installed in Scribner's basement. Artificial turf was spread around the base of the machine, and Dick painted an outdoor mural on the basement walls, so JBS could ride the mechanical horse with some scenery around him. Once again, JBS' brown Rolls Royce made regular trips from town, past *The Western Horseman*, past the Flying Horse and Highfield West to Scribner's place, where he would park the car and go for a "ride."

Dick was still working on the mural one day when JBS was getting ready to return to town. Someone spotted a skunk lurking under the Rolls Royce, and Dick, who always had firearms handy, lay on the ground and took aim at the skunk with a .22. The idea, Dick recalled later, was to hit the skunk on the spine, and that would prevent him from reflexively spraying under the car. Dick fired and all was well. It wasn't till later Dick considered the consequences if his shot had been off even a little. "That would have been a bad thing to happen to that car," he admitted.

Chan and Melitta Bergen, meanwhile, bought 10 acres adjoining the Scribner ranch (and overlooking the Flying Horse) in 1968. They built a beautiful home and stable on the property, which was covered with a blend of scrub oak, grass and pine trees, and acquired a couple of horses. Chan had been on just two horses prior to coming aboard at the magazine. Now he was an enthusiastic trail rider who wrote about various trail rides for *WH*, and also wrote the monthly western-art "Gallery" column.

End of the 1960s

The 1960s wound up with a banner year for the magazine in many ways. The March issue, 1969, had a change in the masthead—Dick Spencer III had been promoted to publisher as Don Flint retired. The rest of the masthead: Chuck King, editor; Chan Bergen, assistant editor; John Harris, advertising director; Hal Bumgardner, production manager, E. Rodney Koht, general manager.

Below that: "*The Western Horseman* is published monthly by Western Horseman Inc., of Colorado Springs, Colorado. John Ben Snow, chairman of board; Don B. Flint, president; Dick Spencer III, vice president; John Harris, secretary; E. Rodney Koht, treasurer. Affiliated with Speidel Newspapers Inc., a national service and research organization devoted to publications in the best interest of our country and our homes."

The editor at that time, Chuck King, dictated a letter to Barbara Emerson, editorial secretary.
WESTERN HORSEMAN ARCHIVES

Christmas greetings from The Western Horseman *to the readers appeared in the December 1969 issue, which included photos of the staff at that time. The article led off with a picture of Dick, who recently had been named publisher. Chan Bergen took the photograph, and the following photos also appeared in that same issue.*
WESTERN HORSEMAN ARCHIVES

When this shot was taken, Chan Bergen was assistant editor. Next to his desk is John Ben Snow's silver-mounted parade saddle, which today is displayed in the John Ben Snow wing of Colorado Springs' Pioneers Museum.
WESTERN HORSEMAN ARCHIVES

Hal Bumgardner, advertising production manager; John Harris, advertising director; and Irene Rayford, advertising traffic manager, often had their heads together.
WESTERN HORSEMAN ARCHIVES

Marilee Cater and Ellen Bushey, circulation secretaries, used a microfilm viewer back then to check subscription orders.
WESTERN HORSEMAN ARCHIVES

Steve Prentice and Pat Close were editorial assistants when this photo was shot.
WESTERN HORSEMAN ARCHIVES

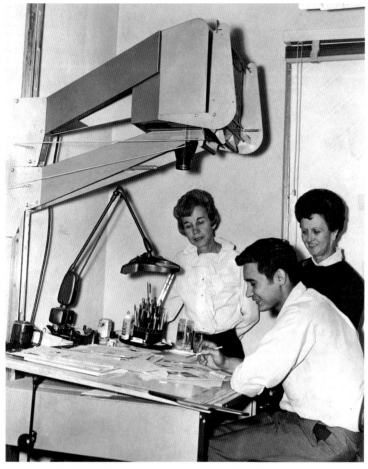

Kay Kuehn, artist in layout and design; Bob Marquez, artist; and Ruth Kendrick, in charge of classified advertising and readership service, were going over an ad layout.
WESTERN HORSEMAN ARCHIVES

Jeanette Pinell, receptionist, posed beside a front-office display of WH books.
WESTERN HORSEMAN ARCHIVES

Howard Barber was in charge of subscription fulfillment, and Gwen Komatz was a clerk in the WH mailroom.
WESTERN HORSEMAN ARCHIVES

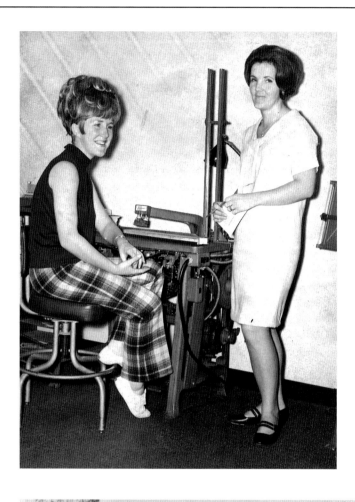

Pat Munson operated the Graphotype, and Sharon Pierce served as circulation clerk.
WESTERN HORSEMAN ARCHIVES

Bill Vollrath, circulation bookkeeper; Eleanor Shepperdson, accountant; and Ralph Lavelett, IBM operator and outgoing mail manager, checked the control panel for an IBM accounting machine.
WESTERN HORSEMAN ARCHIVES

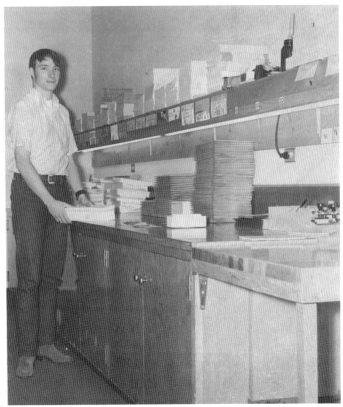

Chuck Lowery, mail clerk, sent out many
Western Horseman *books.*

WESTERN HORSEMAN ARCHIVES

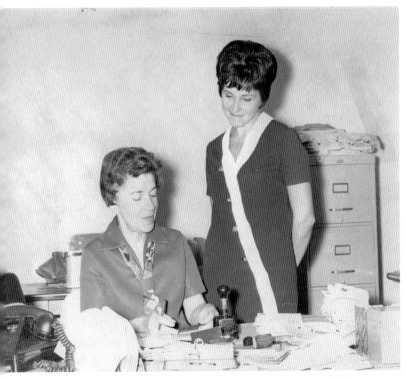

Barbara Connelly was the assistant bookkeeper, and Pat
Hoffman, the circulation typist.

WESTERN HORSEMAN ARCHIVES

Also listed were the magazine's out-of-office advertising representatives: Donald B. Thomson, Bargersville, Indiana; Robert R. Pierson, Chicago, Illinois; March & McCarty, Los Angeles, California.

Subscriptions sold for $5 per year and total circulation was topping 213,000. The May issue—tagged "New Wear and Gear for '69"—was the thickest of the year with a whopping 262 pages.

The December issue included Christmas greetings from the entire staff, with photos of each person, along with job titles. The entire office staff included Dick as publisher; Chuck King, editor; Barbara Emerson, editorial secretary; Chan Bergen, assistant editor; Steve Prentice and Pat Close, editorial assistants; Jeanette Pinell, receptionist; John Harris, advertising director; Hal Bumgardner, advertising production manager; Irene Rayford, advertising traffic manager; Kay Kuehn, layout and design artist; Bob Marquez, artist; Ruth Kendrick, in charge of classified advertising and readership service; Rod Koht, general manager; Bart Marshall, circulation trainee; Marilee Cater and Ellen Bushey, circulation secretaries; Howard Barber, subscription fulfillment; Gwen Komatz, mail room clerk; Bill Vollrath, circulation bookkeeper; Eleanor Shepperdson, accountant; Ralph Lavellet, IBM operator and outgoing mail manager; Barbara Connelly, assistant bookkeeper; Pat Hoffman, circulation typist; Pat Munson, Graphotype operator; Sharon Pierce, circulation clerk; and Chuck Lowery, mail clerk.

Dick Spencer wrote his monthly "Brush Poppin' in the Far West"—a potpourri column containing whatever Dick was interested in writing about. He (and others) would also write a "Just Whittlin'" column that usually voiced opinions about something in the horse industry. Dick used the "Just Whittlin'" column for the following: "Each year about this time Christmas cards start to pour in...from our readers to *The Western Horseman*. We have always appreciated it. We are still amazed that people are friendly and thoughtful enough to take the time to send a Christmas card to a magazine.

"So on that basis, we thought you might like to see the people at work in the home office, where each issue of *The Western Horseman* is foaled. We assure you that we enjoy putting out the magazine, and hope you continue to enjoy reading it...."

Rod Koht was WH *general manager, and Bart Marshall was a trainee in the circulation department at the time.*

Other regular columnists at the time included Chuck King, "Riding the Rimrock;" Robert M. Miller, DVM, "Vet's Corner;" Ruth Schoner, "Western Preview;" Jerry Armstrong, "Rodeo Arena;" and Ray Davis, "Headin' and Heelin'." Between the front and back covers was the usual variety of interesting, entertaining, and informative articles on cowboys, cowgirls, ranching, horse health care, rodeo, trail rides, western clothing and gear, plus stories on individual horses, mules and old-timer personalities.

Among the articles that month was one penned by Chuck King and Chan Bergen, who had accompanied the Cowboy Artists of America on the group's annual trail ride. Good western art appeared on most of the covers by then, and a lot of it was by the professional CAA artists, a close-knit band who appreciated the publicity and encouragement given them by the *WH* during their formation that decade.

Artists George Phippen, Joe Beeler, John Hampton, and Charlie Dye had gotten together in the Oak Creek Tavern in Sedona, Ariz., talked about forming an organization composed of western artists, and then asked Dick Spencer what he thought of the idea. Dick said, "Go to it" and the magazine would give them some publicity. The article appeared in 1964 and John Hampton said afterwards, "... then came the deluge!" After George Phippen died and they had their Cowboy Artists Exhibition at the Cowboy Hall of Fame, the magazine presented the first George Phippen Memorial trophy for the work of art that was most popular in the public's acclaim. So, yes, the magazine and the CAA enjoyed a close relationship.

ICD   08885

The WESTERN HORSEMAN

JANUARY 1976   **75 CENTS**

Since 1936,
The World's Leading
Horse Publication

40th ANNIVERSARY ISSUE

6

THE 1970s

A Decade of Change

The dawn of another decade saw *The Western Horseman* thriving. Circulation would top 230,000 subscribers and newsstand buyers each month. Advertising was strong for horses and horse gear, health products and trailers, western wear for men and women, and dozens of small, miscellaneous products like pocket knives, grooming supplies, belts and buckles, horse treats, hoof nippers, and branding irons.

You could order a life-size fiberglass horse from the ad placed by Bob Prewitt and Alkire's Fiberglass in Billings, Montana—and *WH* acquired one of them and placed it on the lawn in front of the office building. Cecil Dobbin, one of Dick's Appaloosa pals east of town, bought one, too, had it painted to look just like his great Appaloosa sire, Bright Eyes Brother, and invited Dick out to his ranch to see it placed near the front entrance. Dick brought along his camera and recorded the whole ceremony, which appeared in the magazine. Cecil led the stallion out to look at the fiberglass horse. "Brother" sniffed noses with it, then suddenly whirled around and kicked the heck out of the strange intruder!

Ads and Articles

It was easy to get the magazine out each month. Advertising poured in, and so did the articles. Readers would send in their own stories for "their magazine." The manuscripts would often need work, but if there was a good story in it, the editorial staff would take care of any editing or rewriting. A stable of freelance writers also contributed on a regular basis, sending everything they wrote first to *WH,* and whatever *WH* couldn't use would eventually appear in other publications. This is an enviable position for a magazine to be in. *The Western Horseman* didn't pay the highest rates for articles, but the policy was to quickly respond with acceptance or denial, and to pay on acceptance.

Advertising artist Dwayne Brech was serious about a career as a western artist, and he produced this cover painting for the January 1976 issue. Chuck King mentored Dwayne on the subject, explaining how a couple kids out riding might get through a tight wire gate. Dwayne went on to do many more western paintings and drawings for us and for the public.

Horse on the Roof

Here's how the fiberglass horse wound up on the roof. I hadn't worked at *WH* all that long when we all showed up at the office one morning and the horse was found damaged. Vandals had cut him off above the fetlocks—and this was after Howard Barber had concreted his feet into the lawn following a similar act of vandalism.

I was standing in the hallway with Dick and Chan, discussing what we should do to thwart future acts. I spoke up and started to say, "You know, we could put that horse on the roof, but if someone really wants to get him, they'll find a way to climb up on the roof."

Chan cut me off halfway through my non-idea. I got as far as, "You know, we could put that horse on the roof...."

And Chan said, "That's a great idea, Randy!"

That afternoon, Dwaine Poston and I were standing on the edge of the roof, each with a rope in hand attached to the horse, hoisting him up. We anchored him up there and no one ever bothered the fiberglass horse again.

We took a lot of group pictures in front of the building through the years, and this crowd is composed of rodeo clowns! In town one year for a rodeo clown reunion during the Pikes Peak or Bust Rodeo, they all stopped by the office for a visit.

BERT ANDERSON/*WESTERN HORSEMAN* ARCHIVES

Readers had an active role in what appeared in the issues, and professional free-lancers could count on receiving checks in a timely fashion, or at least receiving their manuscripts back quickly in order to submit them elsewhere for consideration. The editorial staff spent most of its time editing manuscripts, proofreading copy, laying out the articles, and perhaps writing a column or two. Each editorial staffer would get to go on a "plum" assignment once a year. That might mean a trip to the National Finals Rodeo for someone like Chuck King, or perhaps a trip to a national horse show or a first-class trail ride for others.

Some articles would be time-sensitive, and they would appear in the next available issue. Others, especially those of a historical nature (old-time cowboy yarns, ranching in years gone by, famous old horses) would be laid out

Vintage Ads

There have been a lot of longtime advertisers in Western Horseman *through the years, and these are some of them.*

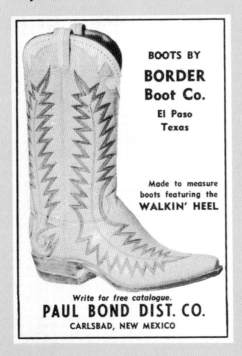

and kept in inventory, ready to be scheduled at any time.

Advertising always determined how many pages would appear in any given issue. A page of advertising would pay for a page of editorial. The formula was pretty much 50-50, advertising and editorial. John Harris, one of the early hires when the magazine came to Colorado Springs, was advertising director at this time. Hal Bumgardner was advertising production manager and therefore responsible for laying out the advertising portion of the "dummy," placing ads throughout the allotted pages.

Chuck King and Chan Bergen worked together on filling out the dummy with editorial articles. Chan would do most of the cut-and-paste. Chuck would schedule most of the articles and then "doodle" on a separate dummy sheet, creating a cartoon that was often based on something funny that had happened to Chan while putting the issue together. Sometimes articles would have to be re-dummied in order to fit properly around whatever ad configuration was presented. Chuck and Chan would drive up to the Hirschfeld Press in Denver with the completed dummy, and another issue would be well underway.

One time, after handing over the dummy to the Hirschfeld crew, a Line-o-type operator walked up to them and said, "Hey, what happened to pages 89, 99,109 (etc.)." The advertising department had accidentally dropped a number of pages, and Chuck and Chan hurried back to the office and went straight to the article cabinet to fill in all the blank pages.

Western Art

Covers continued to feature mostly western art—historical and modern paintings, pictures of bronzes or even woodcarvings—with the occasional photograph, usually something that tied in with a story inside that issue. Covers were selected to be seasonal; for example, snow scenes in winter, spring branding scenes in May or June, something with fall colors in perhaps September, October or November. There was usually a strong horse angle in the art or photos, something that "told a story."

For a painting to make it on the cover the artist had to be accurate in depicting horse type and conformation, plus whatever gear was shown. For example, bridles and saddles

had to be portrayed accurately, and had to fit whatever period was being portrayed in the scene; a horseback scene from the 1800s should not have a modern saddle and bridle.

Hand-In-Hand... Sometimes

The advertising offices ran the length of the upper floor on the north side of the building, while editorial offices occupied our south side. For the most part, advertising and editorial were separate endeavors, sometimes to the detriment of the operation. More than once, a major feature would appear and someone in advertising would say, "Gosh, if I'd only known this story was going to appear, I probably could have sold an ad to...." The two departments would vow to work more closely together after that, only to slip up again from time to time as the years went by.

One place the two departments always have worked hand-in-hand is at the big Denver International Western/English Apparel & Equipment Market, a huge trade show held each January in Denver during the National Western Stock Show. *Western Horseman* and other horse magazines have booths and displays at the show, right alongside hundreds of western and English clothing and equipment manufacturers. The show is closed to the general public, and retail store owners from throughout the country, even the world, converge on the sprawling Denver Merchandise Mart to see what's new and place store orders for the coming year. This is a good time for *WH* personnel to visit with folks who advertise in the magazine, and to promote the latest *WH* books for consideration of store owners to carry.

There was another occurrence in which editorial and advertising worked hand-in-hand, and the result was so good it became a monthly ritual. JBS was still receiving his hand-delivered issues each month, courtesy of Rod Koht, and Rod returned one day with a message from JBS to the editorial department. JBS asked why so many articles had to be continued in the back of the magazine. It was annoying for readers to continually thumb to the back of the magazine after starting a feature article up front, he said. Could more articles run consecutively without being carried over to the back? It was a case of, "We've always done it this way...." The dummy would come to editorial after advertising had pasted up all the ads, separating competitors from one another; it was

WESTERN HORSEMAN®

60th Anniversary Issue 1936-1996

World's Leading Horse ine Since 1936

January 1996
$2.95 U.S.
$3.50 Outside U.S.

Years ago Western Horseman *commissioned George Phippen, founding member and first president of the Cowboy Artists of America, to create three illustrations, which were used in the magazine for a half-century beginning in 1955. This illustration, one of the three, became the 60th anniversary issue cover in January 1996.*

WESTERN HORSEMAN ARCHIVES

always up to editorial to work around whatever configuration advertising presented. Chan went to work on the problem, and the upshot was simply to work together with Hal in advertising, giving Hal a sequence of articles for ads to fit around. The result was a better magazine for everyone.

Sad Times, Too

The 1970s were certainly filled with change, but not all of it was good. On the one hand, John Ben Snow died at age 89 on January 21, 1973, following a brief illness. A few days later, several hundred people gathered in Colorado Springs to pay respects and eulogize him. His death was mourned, yet his life was celebrated as one that had been full and productive. He left in place several philanthropic organizations: The John Ben Snow Foundation, the Snow Family Trust, and the Snow Memorial Trust. He was buried in his hometown of Pulaski, N.Y., and his Western Horseman Inc. stock was purchased by the corporation for redistribution to more employees.

On the other hand, a parent's worst nightmare came true for the Spencers and Kings in the first half of the 1970s. In 1972, Rick Spencer lost an arm when he touched a hot electrical line in an abandoned mining site near Breckenridge. There was a lengthy hospitalization and recovery period, and it seemed Rick had just learned to cope with the disability when he was killed in 1974 while riding with friends in a car that accidentally plunged off a high mountain road. The Spencers were devastated, and Dick spoke occasionally about the painfully slow healing process people go through after such losses.

Then, in 1975, Chuck and Margaret King were at the Grand National Rodeo in San Francisco when they learned their son, Mac, had committed suicide in their home. Chuck and Margaret couldn't stay in the house after that; they needed to get away. The solution was described in the January 1976 issue, in the "Just Whittlin'" column penned by Dick.

"With this issue, which celebrates our 40th year in serving the horse industry," Dick began, "the reins of editorship are officially taken up by Chan Bergen, and Chuck King has moved on with the title of field editor. The editor's job on any magazine is an important one; and his main job is to reach, and please, as many readers as possible. This is an especially big job on a magazine that has as large a field of readers as we do, and with so many varied interests. It's an all-breed magazine, designed to inform and entertain people of all ages who like horses. That's men, women, and youngsters—from beginners to professionals—from remote ranches to big cities—and all the various in-betweens....

"Chuck King will be working out of [Scottsdale] Arizona, but he didn't get off to the flying start he had hoped for. One of his colts blew up on him down there, and Chuck sustained a broken pelvis, so he'll be out of the saddle for awhile. But he'll be back soon gathering material, and his by-line will continue in the magazine." Chuck never fully recovered from his injury, yet he managed to

This is the photo of Chan and his horse used in the magazine when Dick announced that Chan was the new editor and Chuck would serve as field editor in Arizona.

COURTESY CHAN BERGEN

Chuck's Cartoons

Chuck King was a good cartoonist, as well as an illustrator for the magazine. Chan Bergen wound up with quite a collection of Chuck's cartoons that had been drawn just for Chan while the two were pasting up the dummy for the next issue. Chan did the cut and paste while Chuck looked on and offered advice. Chuck invariably would start doodling on a piece of dummy board and create a cartoon based on something recent that had occurred in Chan's life.

These two cartoons depict Chan's horse, Rev. Rev is worried about getting down to one last bale of hay in one, and the other commemorates Chan investing in a stock tank heater. Chuck held out for a long time before he finally tried a tank heater, too. After finally installing a tank heater one winter, he habitually bragged about how little or no ice was on the tank each morning when he came into the office.

CHUCK KING, COURTESY CHAN BERGEN

stay horseback and team rope for the rest of his life, and he contributed many worthwhile "Ridin' the Rimrock" columns and feature articles for years to come.

Dick went on to write that "Chan's by-lined articles over the years past will attest to the scope of his interests and activities in the horse business. And Chan is backed by what we strongly feel is the most competent and enthusiastic editorial department in the horse magazine business…."

The Past 40 Years

In that same issue, Dick included a lengthy article he penned titled "The Past 40 Years in the Horse Business." He wrote that, "Forty years isn't really a long time; yet no other magazine devoted to the western horse exists that was published before that time. There was no Appaloosa Horse Club then, and the American Quarter Horse Association hadn't come into being at that time." Dick wrote that the magazine had been proud to help both the APHC and AQHA—and other breed associations—with advice and publicity during their formative years. "There are still 'old-timers' around who might remember that we showed the founders of the *Quarter Horse Journal* everything we knew about putting out a magazine… editorial, advertising, and circulation. And the *Appaloosa News* can and will tell you how we helped them over the years, even before they had a newsletter…."

Dick hosted a hunting camp each year at his ranch during deer season. Friends were invited to spend a weekend in the bunkhouse, where there was good camaraderie, and occasionally someone would even bag a deer. This shows the deer camp crowd of 1976. Among those pictured with Dick is son-in-law and Associate Editor Kurt Markus, who is kneeling with Dick in front. Chan Bergen is at far right, and next to him are Bill Pennington, a future staffer, and John Harris.

Dick mentioned the magazine had helped in many other ways in the development of the horse industry in the past 40 years—ways in which most people may not have realized—"a trophy each year to the National Appaloosa Show, for years a saddle to one of the Rodeo Cowboys Association champions, trophies for National Little Britches, buckles for the Girls Rodeo Association, horse judging buckles at the Cow Palace, and countless others to different groups and in different categories, even monetary contributions for the 'new' coliseum at the Denver National Western, and to the Cowboy Hall of Fame. Over the years this would make quite a list, but we point it out only because we have been doing it in the background and many people think a magazine's only contribution is through publicity and reporting. And these people may be more right than we are, because in most cases we were the only horse magazine doing this."

Dick traced the history of professional rodeo, and mentioned that *The Western Horseman* was ten months older than organized rodeo, which began with the Boston Garden Strike by cowboys in October 1936. He wrote about the formation of the National Finals Rodeo, the International Finals Rodeo, and how *The Western Horseman* had designed the distinctive gold membership pin of the Rodeo Historical Society, created out of the development of the National Cowboy Hall of Fame. He noted that the RHS always selected a Rodeo Man of the Year, that our own Chuck King was presented this award in 1969, and that our longtime rodeo reporter Jerry Armstrong was the first of 35 charter members of the RHS organization.

There was also mention of some major trail riding groups, and Dick noted that many of these organizations had patterned themselves from the "daddy of 'em all" in trail riding, the Rancheros Visitadores out of Santa Barbara, Calif., which began in 1930 and continues today.

Dick also bragged a bit—justifiably so—about the series of articles the magazine had done to help youngsters with their horsemanship (which led to the book *Beginning Western Horsemanship*), and how the series had won a Maggie Award back in 1958—"which was then to the magazine industry what the Oscar is to motion pictures and the Emmy is to television.... Other Maggie winners that year were *Life, Look, Better Homes and Gardens, Mademoiselle, Good Housekeeping, Sport, Modern Screen,* and *TV Radio Mirror*. A pretty fast track for a little ol' horse magazine!"

Dick also wrote about the growing trend of "horse clinics" around the country. In 1956, the Rocky Mountain Quarter Horse Association asked *WH* to work up some sort of educational program for free presentation at the 1957 Denver National Western Stock Show. It sounded like a good idea, Dick said, and he and others went to work on a motion picture film (color, but no sound), plus slides to help in the veterinary part of the program.

"We didn't know what to call the program, but we had heard of photography clinics and writing clinics," Dick explained in the article, "so we came up with the word 'horse clinic.' We thought it sounded a little 'medical,' but we didn't come up with a better word at the time. The first one packed 2,000 people into inadequate space, and we did it again the following year because of the tremendous response. Ed Honnen, a good promoter for the Rocky Mountain Quarter Horse Association (and later president of AQHA) liked the film idea so well that he instigated the AQHA film program shortly after that, only he did it up right! Both sound and color. Other associations followed up on the idea, and now most of them have some sort of film library available for club or individual use. ... And within a few years there were 'clinics' for just about everything—barrel racing, cutting horses, roping, etc."

That January 1976 issue had an oil painting on the cover done by Dwayne Brech, the up-and-coming young artist who was working in the advertising department at that time, but also working to become an artist. Chuck King had come up with the idea for the painting, and helped Dwayne with the conception of a couple kids, horseback, who had to go through a tight, hard-to-open-and-close wire gate. The painting showed how the kids managed to open and close the gate via a catch rope attached to the gate and dallied to a saddle horn. After the painting was completed by Dwayne, Chuck laughed and said for all the help he had given, the credit line should read: "Painting by Chuck King, brush work by Dwayne Brech."

Gary Vorhes

Among the editorial staff at that time was Gary W. Vorhes, who had joined the magazine in 1970 as a young cowboy-journalist fresh out of the Navy. Gary grew up on the farm in north-central Iowa, and trained a couple colts by reading Dick's *Horse Breaking* book. "I thought I was a helluva cowboy till I made the mistake of leaving Iowa," Gary says with his typical big, rollicking laugh. "The biggest area I was green in was my horse knowledge, and I owe a lot to the people who taught me things along the way. At *The Western Horseman* I learned about the magazine business and horses and the West, and was sure proud to be there. Loved every minute of it."

If Gary was a little green about the horse business when he hired on, he did bring with him a solid background in journalism. He had worked on the newspaper at the University of Iowa and continued to work in journalism throughout his Navy days, which included a stint on the aircraft carrier *Intrepid* during the Vietnam War. At his core, Gary is an old-time newspaperman and reporter who grasps how to ask the right questions, and knows how to edit copy to get rid of extraneous fluff. As the years unfolded, he also became a top horseman himself.

Now in his mid-60s and retired, Gary figures he's still learning. "My education hasn't yet ceased in horsemanship," he said. "As in many other areas, wisdom consists of

Gary and Corliss Vorhes were active trail riders with the Kit Carson Riding Club. This was taken of them in 1981 along the front range of the Colorado Rockies. Corliss, on the palomino, is holding youngest daughter Tara, and Gary and Amy are to the right.

COURTESY GARY VORHES

understanding what you don't know, and I've expanded that to volumes by being around a lot of really good horse people, which is one of the main joys of working at the magazine." It didn't take Gary long to start "living the life" after he began work. Within a handful of months he was in rented quarters adjacent to the barn at Flying Horse Ranch, and had his own horse to ride each evening after work.

Gary also figured out, early on, a key element in the success of the magazine. To wit: "The office floor-tile was always kept clean and shiny," he recalled, "and one morning, after everyone was settled in at their desks and starting to work, someone walking down the hall said, 'Who tracked in this horse manure?'

"We all poked our heads out of our offices, and sure enough, there was a clump of horse manure on that shiny tile floor. Everyone walked into the hall and did what I call The Stork Dance, standing on first one foot then the other to look at the bottoms of their boots. We never determined who the guilty party was, but it reinforced one of my private conceits—that we were a way better horse magazine because we were all involved in our own horse activities. Each of us assumed it could have been us that tracked in the manure, because we all fed horses before we came to work. We weren't magazine people putting out a horse magazine; we were horse people putting out a horse magazine. I've always said the staff was just supporting our own habits, because we all went home and spent way too much money on our own horses and never regretted it."

Corliss Palmer

In the spring of 1972, Advertising Director John Harris needed to fill the position of advertising assistant, and he wound up interviewing and hiring a young woman, Corliss A. Westerbuhr, who had been born in Nebraska, finished growing up in Rawlins, Wyo., and was recently graduated from the University of Wyoming. Corliss was, and is, outgoing and friendly, and has an appreciation for the little humorous things that can occur daily in the work place. She has a spontaneous laugh that proves infectious to those around her.

She was four years younger than Gary, but they were both younger than most people who worked on that floor of the building, so it wasn't surprising that she and Gary started

Here's a portrait of Corliss with her first-born, Amy, who has since followed her parents' lead and become an equine journalist, too.

OLIN MILLS COURTESY CORLISS PALMER

dating. They wound up marrying and that union produced two daughters, Amy and Tara, who seemed to inherit the best traits of both parents and enjoyed growing up with horses a part of the family lifestyle.

"Corliss and I were heavily involved in the Kit Carson Trail Riding Club," Gary said. "She held a number of offices for the outfit; I was playing cowboy polo at the club, and, of course, our daughters grew up at the saddle club. Amy and Tara participated in horse shows, gymkhanas and trail rides; they went to 4-H horsemanship clinics, and it was all a huge part of our lives. The club put on ropings and had a parade unit, so we were involved. We understood the parents trying to get their kids started with horses and how important 4-H is. We realized our kids were better schooled in horsemanship and horse care than we had been. Anyway, we were always pretty close to the horse industry whether at work, at home, or recreationally."

Life is filled with transitions, however, and Gary and Corliss divorced. Corliss eventually remarried and became Corliss Palmer, and Gary left the magazine in 1977 and went to work for *The Colorado Springs Sun,* a local newspaper. He returned to *Western Horseman* in 1986, as an associate editor, again working across the hall from Corliss. Through the years, Corliss and Gary proved there was such a thing as an amicable divorce, and their daughters thrived with continued support of both parents. Both daughters were graduated from Colorado State University, and both are still involved with the horse industry.

I Join *WH*

When Gary left the magazine in 1977, there was a need once more for an associate editor, particularly someone who could write knowledgeably about rodeo. My job query and resumé had languished in the office for about a year when Dick pulled it up and passed it along to Chan as a possibility for the position. I was asked initially to simply write the

monthly "Rodeo Arena" column, on a freelance basis, which I readily agreed to do while still employed by the Professional Rodeo Cowboys Association.

The possible offer of a full-time job never crossed my mind, even when Chan showed up for a personal visit at my office in the Denver PRCA headquarters. When he finally asked if I would be interested in such a position I said yes, but would need to talk it over with my wife, Marsha.

The following week found Marsha and me, and our 5-year-old daughter, Mary Claire, in Chan's office. He explained how the magazine worked and talked about the various benefits. I agreed to take the job—one of the best decisions I would ever make—and asked only to have enough transition time so I didn't leave the PRCA in a bind. I went to the National Finals Rodeo that December, as I had done each of the preceding years since 1970, but this time I was covering it for *The Western Horseman.*

Here's another of the three pieces of Phippen artwork so closely associated with WH *through many of the outfit's 75 years.*

7

In and Out of the Office

A Great Place to Work

I was happy, excited and a little awe-struck the day I reported to work and walked through the big wooden door, past the receptionist desk, past Dick Spencer's office and on down the hall toward Chan's office on the west end of the building. I was close to 30 years old, and for the first time in my life felt like I had a promising career ahead of me. The offices were spacious; the atmosphere was generally quiet aside from the sound of typewriters in use, muted conversation, and laughter from time to time. Soft elevator music was piped through the intercom, which the receptionist also used to page people or notify them of phone calls.

Everyone in the office had electric typewriters —except Dick. He had an old manual and figured that was plenty good enough. There was a new IBM Selectric typewriter waiting for me, and I was impressed. That first day found me working on freelance manuscripts—editing and rewriting where necessary—plus proofreading galleys of type. Chan showed me how to select type styles to go with various article titles.

There was no "art director" in those days, someone responsible for the overall design of each issue. Instead, each editorial staff writer would select a type style for each article he or she worked on, whether it was a freelance piece or one of our own stories. This allowed for a wide range of type styles in each issue, and one of my favorites was called "Log" type. It was a rustic style that looked like letters formed by logs—pretty corny even back then. Chan always remembered the time a reader commented that the magazine had "kind of a homemade look to it" and that he liked it. Maybe he meant "homey."

Typewritten copy and black-and-white photos to be "shot as half-tones" were placed in a wire basket in the editorial secretary's office, and several times a

Here's a picture of Kurt Markus horseback in a "sea of sagebrush" on the old Rancho Idaho (named now as Big Springs Ranch) out of Bruneau, Idaho.

day a courier from a local print shop in town would pick up this material and also leave behind typeset galleys and half-tones, all to be proofed for accuracy and then pasted on layout sheets. The magazine content was still mostly in black-and-white in those days, which meant most of our photos ran in black-and-white. Those we shot for our own articles, we developed and printed ourselves in the office darkroom, a nice set-up with enlarger and developer. The room was in the back of the building, in the new addition between Chan's office and mine.

Our offices were all interconnected, and on the other side of mine was that of Kurt Markus, a West Point graduate who was married to Dick and Jo's youngest daughter, Debbie. Kurt had served in the Army, become interested in journalism, and wound up as an associate editor at the magazine. Beyond Kurt's office was that of the editorial secretary, Gwen Komatz, and then the office of Pat Close, who was also an associate editor

New guy at the Western Horseman—*Randy Witte—who showed up to write about rodeo and other things. Kurt Markus took this mug-shot of me to go with the column head for "Rodeo Arena."*

WESTERN HORSEMAN ARCHIVES

at that time. I enjoyed working with all of them; actually, I liked everyone in the entire *WH* office.

The lower level could be a little noisy when the Address-o-graph machine was punching out names and addresses on the metal plates. Once a month, when the latest issue of the magazine was hot off the press, most of the copies were mailed directly to newsstand wholesalers and subscribers from the printer, located at that time in Lincoln, Nebraska. But a big supply also arrived at the office for special handling. Some readers, especially in foreign countries, paid extra for expedited handling; and new subscribers received special handling until their names were included on the regular subscriber list. If a reader ever phoned and said he never received an issue, another copy would be mailed out that very day. Reader service was high on the priority list.

In-House Humor

Twice a day, at 10 a.m. and 3 p.m., most employees gathered in the coffee room downstairs for a cup of coffee or a soda. The coffee was free, out of a big metal urn that started percolating first thing in the morning. The sodas were dispensed from an antique Coke machine and purchased for 25 cents a bottle, which was cheap even then. Staff members also frequently brought homemade treats or store-bought cookies for everyone to share. This was especially prevalent around the holidays. The only problem was several persons might bring treats on the same day, but then we might go several days without any kind of a sugar fix. Pat Close "solved" this predicament one year when she posted a holiday sign-up sheet for goodies. We had Christmas treats every day throughout December—and most of us gained a lot of unwelcome weight. The coffee room also served as lunch room. Most employees brought their lunches, although Dick and a few others, most notably John Harris and Hal Bumgardner, would often eat out at one of the inexpensive restaurants in the area.

The coffee breaks were great because Dick always showed up for coffee and entertained us with lively jokes or comments on whatever the topic of conversation happened to be that day. One or both local papers were lying on the two long tables, placed end-to-end and surrounded with chairs. One day, Pat Hoffman, one of the best receptionists in the history of the magazine and a veteran of the advertising department, was perusing the Ann Landers column in the *Gazette.* There was a lull in conversation as Pat pushed the column aside and said, almost to herself, "I can't believe Ann Landers today."

"Why not?" Dick asked casually.

Pat, a devoted wife and mother who always radiated a certain sense of wholesomeness and innocence, finished a sip of coffee and said, "Well, her whole column is a warning to young women about all the lame excuses guys have used to persuade them to have sex. Things like, 'If you really love me…' and 'It's good for your complexion….' I just don't think girls are that gullible." She took another sip of coffee and Dick's hand casually slipped over to the newspaper and he pulled it toward himself, glancing down at the Ann Landers column.

Then he said, "Well, I don't know, Pat. This looks like a pretty good list of reasons to me. I'll bet you fell for several of these yourself!"

Pat's mouth fell open and the table generally erupted in laughter. Irene Rayford took a puff on her cigarette and gave Dick the "stink eye." And he just laughed along with everyone else. Dick could get away with things like that. Not everybody could.

One day I related a tale of woe in my personal life—several things had gone from bad to worse, and to top it all off, the septic system had backed up in our house. Dick turned to Chan and said, "You know, if it wasn't for bad luck, Randy would have no luck at all."

Another day in the coffee room and someone commented on yet another article in the paper. A lot of the Vietnam War veterans had never been welcomed home—no outpouring of thanks from the country that had sent them in harm's way. "Well, come to think of it," Chan commented, "no one ever welcomed me home from World War II." (Of course not; the ticker tape parades were all over by the time Chan returned home after a half-year of skiing in Japan.)

But at coffee break the next morning, Chan found in the middle of the table a little green clay sculpture of a soldier, just the head and shoulders, with white beady eyes (literally made with small beads), a simple smile etched on his face, and wearing an old metal concha that looked just like a World War I helmet. A cookie had been placed on the napkin in front of the little soldier, and a toothpick, stuck at an angle into one shoulder of the clay model held a small, hand-printed

St. Patrick's Day

I hadn't worked for *WH* a full year when St. Patrick's Day rolled around. Kurt Markus poked his head in my office and said, "Hey, Randy, it's St. Patrick's Day. We should go down to Murphy's at noon and have one green beer."

Murphy's Tavern was a neighborhood bar down the street about a mile, and as the name might imply, there was a hint of Ireland about the place. I agreed to join Kurt and by the time noon approached, Pat and Dick had decided to join us. We stopped at the deli next door and each got a sandwich, then walked into Murphy's to join the crowd. An elderly man walked past with unkempt hair and beard dyed green.

"Look at that guy," Dick said. "He's been here since last St. Patrick's Day!"

We each had a green beer, and Kurt lifted a couple decorations off the wall—a cardboard leprechaun and a four-leaf clover—to hang in his office as souvenirs. And then we left, simple as that.

A year later, St. Patrick's Day again fell on a weekday, Kurt wanted to go to Murphy's, Pat, Dick and I joined in—and so did about half the rest of the office. A skeleton staff was left behind by default, and we joined the celebrants at Murphy's. Unfortunately, one green beer led to others, and even a little Irish whisky got into the mix.

The afternoon flew by, and the office sent one of the remaining workers to Murphy's with orders to return with the entire crew. That person was quickly caught up in the party and never returned to work. Finally, a second staffer was dispatched with the same orders, and we all made it back to the office in time to go home for the evening, probably just as well because those who had been left behind were in no mood to put up with us.

I think a couple people had to be driven home, and one of our ladies was horrified the next day when she recalled giving her phone number to a stranger at the bar. Dick rationalized our behavior thusly: "Just remember," he said in an Irish brogue, "God created whisky to keep the Irish from rulin' the world!"

It was the last time we celebrated St. Patrick's Day as an office.

sign: "Welcome Home Chan Bergen!" This was Dick's handiwork, of course. "You said you'd never been welcomed home from the war," Dick reminded Chan.

Through the years, the responsibility of putting the flag up the pole and retrieving it each day fell to various persons in the office. For awhile, it was up to Ralph Lavelett. One snowy winter, Ralph had a narrow path shoveled to the flag pole. And on one of those afternoons he rushed out the front door and down the path to get the flag. Unbeknownst to Ralph a number of eyes peered out at him from the windows. Before he got to the flag pole, Ralph suddenly jumped a couple feet in the air and came down looking a little bewildered. There, in the middle of the snowy path, was a coiled rattlesnake—rubber, as it turned out, but courtesy of Dick.

Lots of things happened on a daily basis. Visitors once walked through the door and were greeted by rubber vomit on the floor. Despite the shenanigans, however, the magazine always got to the printer on time. Once a month, a courier from the printing company in Lincoln flew to Colorado Springs to pick up the completed dummy. Chan would go over a few things with him, then the man would fly back to Lincoln with the boxed-up dummy of the next issue.

One Afternoon...

It took nearly a year, but Marsha, Mary Claire and I got settled in a modest house with 13 acres and an adjacent horse pasture for rent near the little town of Monument, a short drive north of the office. We had a handful of horses from Marsha's folks' ranch,

Through the years, the "Here's How" tips proved popular with readers. This how-to idea, one of many compiled in the WH book Helpful Hints for Horsemen, *came from Charlie Carrel, a talented horseman and one-time member of the magazine staff.*

Browband Knot

FROM THE SHOW RING to the roping arena, the crisscross browband knot is popular. It's often seen with silver or horsehair ends, and it can really dress up your headstall. The knot is functional, too, because it makes your browband adjustable.

You can't use your existing browband because it won't be long enough. Instead, you'll need two pieces of leather attached to the long part of your headstall, with a slit cut in one of the pieces. Pass the end of the other piece through the slit, and loop each end over the back of the browband, tucking the ends through.

It's a good idea to leave the ends uncut until you have completed the knot. That way you can be sure they're even and the correct length.

— Charlie Carrel
Sheridan, Wyoming

and these included some mares and a foal; I hauled the foal into the office stable when it came time to wean her. The little filly hadn't been worked with and I needed to get her halter-broke, so Dick helped me.

I'll never forget the afternoon one day after work when he and I started in with the filly. We got her in a stall and Dick eased up to her with a little halter, moving slowly and talking softly. He eased on the halter, then took it off—on and off several times. "Look at her lick her lips," he said, "a sign she's starting to relax." A few weeks later the filly was the subject of a short "Here's How" column Dick did on one aspect of halter-breaking. Kurt Markus took the pictures.

I enjoyed working with Kurt, and since his desk was close to mine it was easy to banter back and forth with each other during the course of a day. Kurt had come to work in December 1975 and quickly proved capable of good writing, editing and photography. He and I worked together on various projects—articles and books, too, as the years unfolded. The first full year I was there we teamed up to do a two-part article on the teenage roping sensation, J.D. Yates. I did the writing, Kurt took pictures. He invested in his own high-quality (and expensive) cameras, and studied techniques of other top photographers.

The Great Basin Revival

Through the course of a few years, Kurt determined there was a part of the West that largely had been overlooked—the Great Basin ranches, home of the buckaroos in the ION country (Idaho, Oregon, Nevada). He was right, too. Visiting a lot of those ranches seemed like stepping back in time—they still used chuck wagons to feed hungry crews for weeks at a time, gathering and branding cattle. The buckaroos slept in old-time bedrolls in traditional tepees. And the crews' horse herd, the *remuda*, was trailed along with the wagon and thrown into a rope corral

This is an early Kurt Markus ranch photo, one he took on the MC Ranch for his feature article on the outfit, which appeared in the July 1979 issue. Titled "Buckarooing on the MC," the story gained widespread popularity and led to more articles on big ranches throughout the West.

KURT MARKUS

Here's a photo of Kurt Markus (taken after he had left WH) at the Bell Ranch in New Mexico. Kurt was born and raised in Montana, but he really became a part of the West when he started photographing the big ranches, riding out with the buckaroos and recording their lives and times for posterity. A lot of folks in Elko know him personally or by reputation.

NICOLE TAVENNER

absentee, had nothing to gain by allowing "the press" on their properties to take pictures, write something possibly foolish, and probably get in the way of whatever work was taking place. Very few persons at that time had been invited to ride with the buckaroos and take photos, but two who had were Bank Langmore and Jay Dusard, both cowboy photographers who could be trusted not only to take great pictures of the range life, but also to not get in the way and not get themselves killed. Langmore and Dusard became friends and mentors to Kurt, who saw to it their work was published in the magazine.

Kurt made a lot of phone calls, wrote a lot of letters, and finally gained the trust of those who owned or otherwise ran these big outfits. The first in a series of epic features Kurt did—both writing and photography—was titled "Buckarooing on the MC," a story and photos about Oregon's MC Ranch buckaroos moving 1,600 head of cattle 70 miles. The article appeared in the July 1979 issue. After that, Kurt and *The Western Horseman* would be welcomed on a lot more of these ranches in the years ahead.

Editorial Travel and Art

The editorial staff was traveling more at this time, going out not only on ranch and rodeo stories, but also to big horse shows, other horse events, interviewing breeders and trainers who had made reputations for themselves. Pat Close wrote a memorable article on legendary horse breeder Hank Wiescamp about this same time, the late '70s; Kurt took the photos. Pat also did a two-part series, "A Coward Breaks a Filly," showing in words and pictures (by Kurt) how she broke her own 2-year-old filly.

Besides going to places like the National Finals Rodeo and Cheyenne Frontier Days, I traveled to events like the big OS Ranch Roping at Post, Texas; the American Junior Rodeo Association Finals in Snyder, Texas; the International Finals Rodeo in Tulsa; and interviewed rodeo champs young and old. Chan made arrangements for me to join the Cowboy Artists of America on a Longhorn drive at the famous YO Ranch near Kerrville, Texas, and I became acquainted with that prestigious group of artists. That same year I did an article on the Bonham Ranch, owned by Marsha's aunt and uncle, Biddy and Wayne Bonham, near Cheyenne.

early each morning, where individual horses were roped out and handed off one by one to the buckaroos.

It was a writer-photographer's dream, filled with tough horses that would buck a guy off, wild cattle, beautiful wide-open country, colorful characters, smoke, blood, dust, rain and snow. The pictures alone could take your breath away. The only problem was gaining access to these ranches. The owners, be they families, corporations or otherwise

Dick is shown here on the Range Ride with one of his longtime pals, Hugh Ingles.
COURTESY SPENCER FAMILY

Supporting our daughter, Mary Claire, in her horse show endeavors was our main family activity—even after she was grown and married. We had this picture taken at the 2004 AQHA World Championship Quarter Horse Show. Mary is on a "family member," Hot Roddin Along, who years earlier had also taken WH writer Juli Thorson to the World Show. Also pictured are friend and horse trainer Sarah Clymer, Marsha and me, and Mary's husband, Trey Niemeyer.

KC MONTGOMERY

We all went to Grover, Colo., for the annual Earl Anderson Memorial Rodeo in June 1978. By "all" I mean Kurt and Debbie Markus, Chan and Melitta Bergen, Marsha, Mary Claire and I. They wanted to see me compete in the last rodeo I would ever enter, and as usual, I was among the losers. We had a good time just the same, and Kurt Markus snapped this picture of young daughter Mary Claire and me after the rodeo.

KURT MARKUS

In those days, the *WH* art gallery was also open for business in the office hallway. Chan was writing the "Gallery" column, giving publicity to aspiring, as well as established western artists, and also listing various pieces of art for sale. Artists sent oil and watercolor paintings, as well as bronzes, all of which would be displayed in the hall for everyone to enjoy. Prices were attached to the various works, and Chan publicized something for sale in each issue of the magazine. The magazine would take a modest commission on anything that sold. We never did a big

business in this endeavor, but had a great time receiving and shipping out paintings and bronzes. A local art hound, Tony Baratono, stopped by almost daily for coffee and supplied some of the art for sale, too.

Longtime Freelancers

There were other regular visitors to the office, including an old cowboy and freelancer named Bob Hewitt, who furnished us with various historical articles and often showed up with a woodcarving or two. He once showed Dick and Chan a carving he had done of a Longhorn steer, then asked Chan, "What else should I do now?"

Chan jokingly suggested an epic woodcarving depicting "10,000 head coming up the trail." Bob took offense, but only for a little while, then got over it.

The loyal freelancers we had then were almost like staff. Lynda Bloom from California sent a lot of practical how-to articles; Robert M. Miller, DVM, also from California, kept us in veterinary articles. Jimmie Hurley of Idaho and Barbara Brown of Denver rounded out our source of rodeo manuscripts, and Texan Barney Nelson became a great source for more ranch stories, as did Buster McLaury, a cowboy who grew up on the famous 6666 Ranch in Texas. Joyce White, a ranch wife from Arizona, periodically sent in interesting ranch and ranch-cooking articles, and, of course, there was the one and only Stella Hughes, renowned chuck-wagon cook and ranch wife to Mack Hughes, longtime manager of the San Carlos Apache Indian cattle operation in eastern Arizona. Stella furnished a lot of entertaining, sometimes wild or even touching, ranch stories. And her stories about various old-time cooks and cooking methods, plus recipes, made her a favorite with readers. Later on, we received more great ranch articles from Mike Laughlin and Lee Raine, an ION couple who both are "the real deal" when it comes to knowing their ways around horses, cattle, cowboys and buckaroos. Even Dick's daughter, Bobbi Jo, had more than 1,500 cartoons published through the years, all featuring "Fizz Bomb," a childproof, user-friendly Appaloosa.

Meanwhile, I was still learning about things other than rodeo, and found it all interesting and entertaining. Marsha helped me a lot because of her ranch and horse

Stella Hughes' column was a favorite with magazine readers for many years, and her chuck-wagon cookbook with her insightful ranch-wife comments continues to sell well.

WESTERN HORSEMAN ARCHIVES

background. Her grandfather, Marshall Peavy, had been an American Quarter Horse Association founder, and her grandmother, Mavis Peavy, was inducted into the Appaloosa Hall of Fame. Mike and Mary Stees, her parents, had raised Quarter Horses and Appaloosas, as well as Hereford cattle on their ranch along Deep Creek, northwest of Steamboat Springs. Marsha and I raised a few foals and got Mary Claire started in the county 4-H horse program. Mary wound up being involved with various horse activities from then on. It's what we did as a family all the years she was growing up.

Bobbi Jo Spencer became a major contributor to WH with her long-running series of Fizz Bomb cartoons, which always featured a little girl and her horse, Fizz Bomb, who was patterned after one of the family horses.
WESTERN HORSEMAN ARCHIVES

• "He's trying to make himself disappear into the corner, so he won't hafta go out riding in the cold weather!"

• "Fizz Bomb, I don't know how tall you are. You're either 16 hands at the withers or 14 hands at the swayback!"

• "You look so much like a shag carpet I don't know whether to ride you or walk on you."

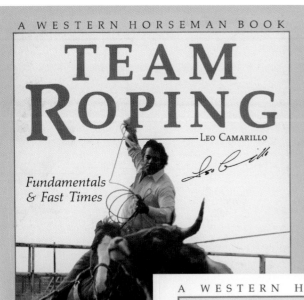

A WESTERN HORSEMAN BOOK

TEAM ROPING

Leo Camarillo

Fundamentals & Fast Times

Featuring: Equipment / Heading / Heeling /

A WESTERN HORSEMAN BOOK

CALF ROPING

Roy Cooper

The World Champion's Guide for Win

A WESTERN HORSEMAN BOOK

Fast Turn-Arounds
Smooth Circles & Long Slides

REINING

Al Dunning

The Complete Guide for Training & Showing the Classic Reining Horse

8

"AS THE WORLD TURNS"

Life at the Opera

We used to laugh that someone could write a soap opera about life behind the scenes at *Western Horseman,* but it would seem too far-fetched for anyone to put up with it. There was death and divorce, a certain amount of jockeying for position among the departments, bad business decisions from time to time, and plenty of laughs from the top. There was also genuine loyalty to the magazine from most of those who worked there.

The backdrop for this era, the 1980s, was the fact that circulation was slipping steadily—not plummeting, but each year since the record of 231,330 subscribers and newsstand buyers, set in December 1972, the figures continued downward. Dick explained that the universe of horse-minded readers was only so big, and that more and more equine magazines had come along in recent years, trying to specialize in one of the many areas our magazine covered, and the result was a certain number of readers would switch to one of the other magazines. For example, someone interested mainly in equine

health care might prefer reading *Equus,* which specialized in that subject. "We should tell those people, once you get your horse well, we'll show you what to do with him," Dick would say. With more publications in the field, there was also more competition for advertising dollars. The staff worked for fairly modest salaries, and when the magazine did well, we all did well through a profit-sharing plan. I think a lot of us felt financially pinched at the time.

Dick's philosophy of maintaining course, steady as she goes, when it came to content and style of the magazine, was well-founded, but met with a certain amount of skepticism among younger members of the editorial staff, especially Dick's son-in-law, Kurt Markus. Kurt wanted to see more and bigger photos in the magazine, he wanted to spend more time in the Great Basin, recording life on those big ranches, and he didn't mind spending more money to improve the magazine's appeal. Kurt would buy black-and-white and color film by the "brick"— which was a lot of film—when he prepared for a trip.

Team Roping with Leo Camarillo *was the first book we did in the "new series" of* WH *titles.* **Calf Roping with Roy Cooper** *and* **Reining with Al Dunning** *quickly followed. Each book always was "spearheaded" by one of the editorial staffers.*

For years, WH had an annual calendar filled with cover art that had appeared on past issues of the magazine. Kurt came up with a new calendar format that featured photos he had taken on big ranches. The new calendar was expensive to produce, but the readers loved it.

WESTERN HORSEMAN ARCHIVES

I know that alone rankled Dick, who might leave on a trail ride with a couple rolls of film in his pocket.

Kurt was assistant editor by then, so he was being groomed to take over the editor's job when Chan retired. Kurt designed a revised *Western Horseman* calendar format—called The Cowboy Calendar—filled with his photos, and pretty expensive to produce. It replaced the traditional *Western Horseman* calendar offered each year, and became a popular item among readers. Kurt always took plenty of close-up gear pictures—boots and spurs, chaps and so forth. At that time, chinks—the shorter version of chaps—were common in the ION, but not so common elsewhere. Same with the packer, or lace-up, boots. After these and other gear items received widespread attention in the magazine, they started showing up throughout the country.

Instructional Photography

Kurt's photography skills also were used in a new series of *Western Horseman* books. The old books, going back to Dick's *Beginning Western Horsemanship*, needed to be replaced. They were simply out-of-date.

The first book to be replaced was the one on team roping, and that became my project. The magazine always had adhered to the philosophy that a how-to book done with a person acknowledged to be the best in that field was the way to go. The absolute best team roper at that time was Leo Camarillo, the Lockeford, Calif., cowboy who, along with brother Jerold and cousin Reg Camarillo, revolutionized this rodeo event in the 1970s and 1980s, repeatedly winning the National Finals Rodeo and the world championships in pro rodeo. Like many top athletes, Leo was a hard-driving man in his prime, filled with interesting nuances. We agreed to do the book on a handshake, then I followed him around for three days, not getting anything done on the book. I was beginning to panic, thinking I might return to the office with nothing to show for my trip. Finally, after returning to the Camarillo home after a run to the Reno rodeo, Leo sat down with me and gave me one of the best interviews I've ever had. Kurt and I flew back out that fall when Kurt took the instructional photos of Leo and Reg roping steer after steer in Leo's home arena, and the book was a best-seller for *Western Horseman*.

I snapped this photo of Kurt on the scissors lift with Roy Cooper, right after we had finished taking photos of Roy roping in his home arena for the calf-roping book.

WESTERN HORSEMAN ARCHIVES

I did a calf roping book with the sensational champion Roy Cooper, and it, too, was a hit with readers. By then, Kurt had taken to using a lofty "scissors lift" for part of his instructional photography. He would operate the rental device to its full height inside the arena, and the small platform would sway in the breeze while he took overhead photos. I went up with him once and didn't care for the feeling, so stayed on the ground after that.

At least this was an improvement over the giant forklift he rented to take pictures of Al Dunning for the reining book Pat Close did with Al. A sheet of plywood was secured to the forklift, and Kurt stood on it while a friend, Mike Craig, operated the lift, raising it slowly. When it reached its full height, about 15 feet above ground, Kurt asked Mike to ease his "platform" forward.

Pat, who was standing beside the forklift, suddenly noticed the back tires rising off the ground. She hollered at Mike to bring the platform back, but it was too late. The forklift, overbalanced to the front, came crashing down.

Kurt hung on—and amazingly was not hurt except for a bloody forehead where his camera slammed into him. But the forklift was lying useless on the ground. The rental company had to send another forklift to pick up the first one, which—also amazingly—was not damaged.

Transitions

Meanwhile, on the domestic front, Debbie served Kurt with divorce papers upon his return from one of many trips to the Great Basin. And Dick divorced Jo and married Vivian King, a lady who had roots in Great Basin ranching and had come to work in the bookkeeping department at *Western Horseman*. Kurt needed a place to live, temporarily, so he came to stay with Marsha, Mary Claire and me in our house, which had a basement apartment. Kurt and Debbie's beautiful little daughter, Jessica Jo, would visit her dad at our place from time to time.

This is a 1983 photo of Jo Spencer, a beautiful lady inside and out.
OLAN MILLS, COURTESY SPENCER FAMILY

Dick and Viv wound up buying a house and acreage across the road from Chan and Melitta's place, and Jo Spencer continued to live in the original Spencer home.

By this time, Don Wood, one of Dick's longtime friends from the printing business, already had come aboard as advertising director, replacing John Harris, who had retired from his position in 1982. The whole magazine had mourned the death of John's advertising associate, Hal Bumgardner, the previous year. Hal had died prematurely of a brain tumor, and this no doubt influenced John to retire sooner rather than later when reminded of life's tenuous nature.

In those days, summer was heralded with the arrival of Chuck and Margaret King. Chuck and Margaret enjoyed spending all but the hot summer months in Arizona, where Chuck plied his trade as field editor and team roper. But the Kings came to Colorado in the summer, along with Chuck's team roping horse, and Chuck would hang out in the office during much of the day, then rope later in the afternoon and evening.

One summer, Chuck taught a handful of us to rope. We worked out on heading and heeling dummies set up in the parking lot outside the office. Chuck liked to play around with a small kid's rope inside the office, and practiced heeling chairs and roping a doorknob on the backside of an open door. There was a trick to this catch. Chuck would either spin the butterfly loop and have it twist in the air and settle gracefully around the knob behind the door, or it might be more of a straightforward shot, bouncing the loop off the wall and around the doorknob. Chuck would perform this a few times, then challenge anyone working nearby to try the same shot.

One day, Chuck, Kurt and I were wasting time with this activity when Chan walked through, rather briskly, on the way to his office. Chan was obviously preoccupied with something involving actual work for the magazine, but Chuck insisted on stopping him and sticking the rope in his hand, demanding he take a shot at the doorknob. Chan quickly and casually tossed the entire rope in the direction of the door—and the loop miraculously settled neatly around the knob as Chan continued walking toward his office. Chuck just shook his head, and Kurt and I went back to work.

In February 1984, Rod Koht retired after working nearly 35 years for the magazine. He

A Sampling of Dick Spencer Cartoons

LORD, WHEN I PRAYED FER STIRRUP-DEEP GRASS... THIS AIN'T WHUT I HAD IN MIND!

"I PAID MY STALL FEE ... GOT ENTERED IN ALL MY EVENTS... ORDERED STRAW, HAY, AN' GRAIN--- AN' FORGOT WHERE I LEFT MY HORSE!"

"I MEASURED HIM.....HE'S ONLY NINE HANDS!"

and his wife, Helen, were now free to spend more time with children and grandchildren, and Rod would play a lot of golf in Arizona each winter. He was a major stockholder, after serving as circulation manager and then general manager of the company, and the board had to mortgage the office building to buy back his stock. Bart Marshall, the circulation director, took Rod's position, and his title was business manager. A young man, Dwaine Poston, became circulation manager.

That fall, Chan announced his retirement as editor and president of Western Horseman Inc., effective the end of the year. Kurt would take over as editor, starting with the January 1985 issue. We worked two months ahead, so the staff began work on that January issue in November.

Kurt began working with the editorial staff, planning the issue—mostly behind closed doors. This had to bother Dick, but he said nothing. Finally, the day came when Dick took a look at the final January proofs, while Pat was going over them in her office. This was shortly before it was to go to press. A lot of changes in format, use of color, and writing style had been made, an editorial announced future changes, and Dick wasn't happy. To top it off, Kurt wound up writing a letter to the board, outlining his desire for more autonomy over the editorial product, then left for his home, which by then was in the Black Forest, northeast of Colorado Springs.

He Raised Hell!

Dick called the editorial staff into his office and realigned our thinking. For a guy who was so quick with a joke or funny comment, Dick also could look someone in the eye and tell him in no uncertain terms about the error of his ways. He raised hell with us! And we left Dick's office that afternoon in a somber mood. I phoned Kurt that evening, advising him to return to work and tear up his letter. "From what Dick said, I think he might fire you and make me editor if you don't reconsider," I told him.

Kurt didn't reconsider, wished me well, and made an amicable departure from the office. Chan stayed on in an advisory capacity for the board and specifically to help me get my feet on the ground in the editor's office. Kurt continued on his own to take photographs of cowboys and buckaroos, producing a couple of beautiful coffee-table books in the process, and then became

a top professional photographer who, to this day, takes all types of pictures on assignment around the world. He and his wife, Maria, raised two sons, Westin Montana and Ian Nevada, and daughter Jessica Jo, who now goes by the name Jade, often assists him with his photography business.

One might reasonably ask why Pat Close wasn't made editor, instead of me. She was certainly qualified and had more seniority. The answer, of course, is that there was a glass ceiling in *Western Horseman* at that time, just as there were glass ceilings in many other businesses. I don't think the term "glass ceiling" had even been coined at that time, but Pat became managing editor. Dick told her this was a cowboy magazine and we needed a man as editor.

Changes for the Better

Our circulation in 1985 was around 155,000, and that year it began a slow, steady growth. Later, Chan and I both attributed the turnaround to the big-ranch articles and photos Kurt had pioneered for us, and which we continued running as years went by.

I was editor, and also was put on the board of directors. A modest sum of stock had recently been assigned to me, and now I also served as secretary for the board. The board meetings were usually entertaining. We directors sat around Dick's office, talked about one thing and another, and Dick made some humorous remarks.

I've got to hand it to Don Wood, who also was a director. Don always was trying to drag the company into the modern world with various proposals for new staff or equipment. If it involved spending money, Dick was likely to give it thumbs down, at least initially. At one meeting, Don told about the advantages of owning a new piece of equipment called a FAX machine. "A lot of companies have them, and I really think we would use it more than you'd guess," he said.

Dick took a puff on his pipe. "Well, I still think you can get a lot of business done through the mail," he mused. "And we can always pick up a phone...." He asked again what the bottom line price was for a FAX machine, and finally agreed we could get one.

Years earlier, Chan had looked into some of the new computerized typesetting machines that were coming out, and rightfully advised Dick to hold off till the technology leveled off. Eventually, the time came

Dwayne Brech painted some nice cover scenes for the magazine through the years, and we also prevailed upon him to provide artwork for a series of Western Horseman prints we made available to the readers. We also used these fine-art prints as awards to winners in various horse events WH helped sponsor. This beautiful waterfall scene was one of the prints in this series.

DWAYNE BRECH

for us to acquire our own typesetting equipment, and to inch into the computer age. Don convinced Dick and the rest of the board to proceed with this project. We started off with keyboards, screens, and floppy disks. Dick stayed with his manual typewriter, and we simply inputted his column or articles each month. Don also instigated our own production department, which produced the finished page negatives that went directly to the printer, and put his son, Rick Wood, in charge of this department.

By now our printer was World Color Press, one of the biggest and best of the magazine presses, and "our" plant was located in Covington, Tennessee. We enjoyed a warm and productive relationship with Jeff Circuit, our printer representative at World Color. It was Jeff's job to help insure the best possible reproduction of the magazine at the plant, and to make sure contracts were fair both for World Color and for *Western Horseman.* He was paid by World Color, but worked equally hard for us, coming up with various ways to save money without compromising quality. For example, to save postage, World Color devised a way for our magazine to be co-mingled with many other magazine titles they printed. The magazines were shipped reasonably in bulk to various points, where they were separated for delivery to subscribers and wholesalers.

Being editor was fun. There were always article manuscripts to read and decide whether to buy, freelance writers to confer with, staff articles to peruse and help edit, cover art to consider. About the time Kurt was preparing to take over as editor, our "resident artist" Dwayne Brech was transferred from the advertising department to editorial. What a great move that was for the magazine. Dwayne brought greater continuity to the magazine layout and design, painted covers for us from time to time, and served as a well-liked liaison to the Cowboy Artists of America.

When Kurt left, I contacted Darrell Arnold, who had written some good articles for the magazine in the past, and seemed handy with a camera. Darrell had grown up around the scenic little town of LaVeta, in southern Colorado, had an affinity for ranch life and had spent time as a professional packer, taking people into wilderness areas on horseback He was a good fit at *Western Horseman* as an associate editor, capable of going out on ranch stories and taking great pictures. Darrell also enjoyed cowboy poetry and western music, and these topics became a growing niche at the magazine.

In 1987, Gary Vorhes returned to the fold as an associate editor after helping write the final articles and headlines for the *Sun* newspaper, which closed its doors. A local freelance writer, Gavin Ehringer, also became a monthly contributor about this time. We had a strong editorial staff, a rising circulation, and growing advertising.

Our national advertising was handled by Karaban Labiner and Associates in New York City, and with Bruce Karaban at the helm, the company was doing a great job for us. We worked closely with Bruce and his staff, and enjoyed annual sales conferences with them. These were usually tied into a horse activity, like a mountain trail ride, to further acquaint some of the city-bound KLA staffers with firsthand horse experiences. Ensuing years found us making trips to New York City, too, both to meet with the KLA people and International Circulation Distributors, the folks who arranged with individual wholesalers to place *Western Horseman* on newsstands throughout the country. Somehow, it always seemed like a little personal contact with faraway associates was well worth the effort and expense.

Some Mistakes

We made a few business mistakes through the years, usually when we tried to expand our horizons too much beyond the magazine. Certainly we helped pioneer equine books and videos. But there were also a couple real estate ventures in which we even considered relocating our office a couple times, but didn't. We knew how to publish the best horse magazine in the world, but beyond that, we didn't know so much.

In later years we came out with a special "13th issue"—a buying guide for all kinds of horse products—but discontinued it after three years. The guide was successful, financially, but we found no one needed a new guide every year. We also tied in with a local television producer to put *Western Horseman* on TV, a 30-minute program that followed our magazine format. The pilot programs were pretty well done, and I still think the idea is good, but it became obvious that to continue beyond a pilot program would cost more money than we were willing to gamble.

Our resident artist and WH Art Director Dwayne Brech painted this scene of Mike Laughlin hauling trail repair material in the mountains near Estes Park, Colorado. The painting, featured on the February 1997 cover, provided some great art for the magazine, and the original now hangs in my living room. Wife Marsha arranged to buy it from Dwayne and gave it to me for Christmas one year.

DWAYNE BRECH

Relief From Weighty Decisions

Fortunately, these and other weighty decisions always could be set aside at day's end, especially for those of us fortunate to have our own horses. Just like our readers, we could go home and do something with our horses, and the day usually ended well. Going out on assignment for the

I took this photo of Dick with Bill Pennington at the edge of the Cage Ranch cattle pens, the day we flew out to help with branding.

WESTERN HORSEMAN ARCHIVES

magazine—horseback—either on a ranch story or pack trip, was also special. I remember an interesting trip Dick arranged for me in Guadalajara, Mexico, in which I covered the Charro Championships, and as a sidelight took in a bullfight, a livestock show and cattle sale, and wound up horseback in a brushy pasture filled with Mexican fighting cattle.

There was also a memorable visit to a ranch in eastern Colorado, owned by Claude Cage, who had his own twin-engine plane available for our use at the Colorado Springs airport. One of Dick's longtime friends, Bill Pennington, retired Air Force colonel and pilot, was heading up our *Western Horseman* line of products for sale in the magazine at the time, and he piloted the plane that day for Dick, Darrell, Dwayne and me. Bill landed us on a county road near the ranch house, then we "helped" Claude and his ranch crew gather a herd of cows and calves—by helicopter. Claude piloted the open, two-seater helicopter and we took turns riding with him; he would swoop down near the cattle, and the cows would move away from the helicopter. He landed near a clump of brush while I was riding with him, picked up a small calf that had been left behind, and placed the calf in my lap.

"Hold him tight," Claude advised. I maintained a death grip on the calf till we caught up with the herd and got him with his mother. I did a story on the trip—and a few readers complained about the idea of gathering cattle by any other means than horseback.

Pat and I joined Dick and Vivian Spencer on a great pack trip hosted by Cade and Mona Benson, longtime *Western Horseman* friends, in the Colorado Flat Tops, a wilderness area. We took our own horses, and the Bensons packed in all the supplies with a string of mules. Pat did a cover feature for the magazine.

Perhaps the best horseback trip of them all, for me, occurred years later, in 1998, when Jim Jennings, the editor of *Quarter Horse Journal*; Darrell Dodds, the editor of *Paint Horse Journal* (and the future publisher of *Western Horseman*); and I joined an old pal in the printing business, Morgan Lightfoot, for a journey into Mexico.

We started in Lajitas, Texas, on the banks of the Rio Grande, and joined our guide and hostess Linda Walker in the Chihuahuan Desert, a big, wide-open country. We spent several days riding and camping, exploring an

One of the best horseback trips I ever made was into the Chihuahuan Desert with three pals and a great guide, Linda Walker, who snapped this picture of the rest of us at a little waterfall and creek named Milagro (miracle). That's me to the left, then Jim Jennings, editor of Quarter Horse Journal, *Morgan Lightfoot, of Brown Printing Co., and Darrell Dodds, editor of* Paint Horse Journal, *and future publisher of* Western Horseman.

LINDA WALKER

old deserted village and the pristine warm-water San Carlos Canyon. At one point we followed an ancient trail that had been worn into rock. I wrote about the trip in the August 1998 issue.

Dick's Death

In early 1989, Dick became ill. We all figured it was the flu or something, but a couple weeks passed and Dick still couldn't get into the office. Finally, he went to Penrose Hospital in the Springs and tests revealed he had something awry with his pancreas. The ensuing operation showed he had terminal pancreatic cancer, and was given six months to a year to live. Dick went home and received a steady stream of visitors, even though he didn't want his illness to be revealed publicly. Darrell even "ghost-wrote" his column for the magazine, toward the end.

Chan stayed close to Dick; he walked across the road from his house to the Spencers each day, and the two visited and watched various World War II videos. Dick continued to tell jokes to those who came to call. I was there the day retired astronaut Wally Schirra stopped to visit. He and Dick traded jokes, and Wally then departed for the Space Symposium, which was going on in town that week.

The realization that Dick was leaving us threw the office into a fair amount of turmoil. Dick sensed this, and he and Chan conferred. I became assistant to the publisher, as well as editor, and this paved the way for me to become publisher upon Dick's death.

Marsha, Mary Claire and I were in Santa Fe, N.M., where Mary Claire was riding with the Pikes Peak Rangerettes drill team at the rodeo when I got the call that Dick had died on July 15. Services were subsequently held at a park in the Black Forest, and it was quite an occasion. Hundreds of people showed up, including Baxter Black plus the Pikes Peak Range Riders. Among the Range Riders was Chuck Hughes, who led Dick's last horse, a nice-looking gray, saddled and with Dick's boots turned backwards in the stirrups. The September 1989 issue featured a cover photo of Dick, horseback, and the only cover blurb

read "Dick Spencer, 1921-1989." Inside was a lengthy feature article on his life, written by the staff.

Friends and family took part of Dick's ashes horseback up to the Pancakes, the rock formation near Cripple Creek where Harry S. Bunker's ashes had been scattered years earlier. Dick's ashes were buried nearby, and a nice metal cross was placed in the ground. The cross had been made by a fellow Range Rider, John Skalla.

Shortly before Dick died, Pat and I visited Don Flint in his home, which was located in a gated community on the west side of town. We had never been to Don's house before, and were a little surprised to see it filled with Chinese art and furniture, which Don and his late wife had collected for many years. Still, it seemed a bit strange not to find anything that would have commemorated his years with the Flying Horse Ranch or the magazine.

Don was on oxygen. We had a short, pleasant conversation with him, and he answered a few historical questions we had about the magazine. We departed, and Don passed away on October 6. We didn't know his exact birthday, but did know he had been born in 1900 at the turn of the century.

Dick's funeral had been a community event. By contrast there were only a handful of people who attended Don's memorial service, and these included several of us from the office. Don and Florence never had children, and he had been a bit of a recluse in his old age. The service was held in St. Michael's Episcopal Church a few miles north of the office, a church the Flints had helped found back in the 1950s. Even the attending priest conducting the service admitted he hadn't known Don until shortly before his death. When the priest had learned of Don and his condition, he had gone to visit Don and learn something about his life.

"Oh, I'm just an old curmudgeon," the good father quoted Don as saying.

Then the priest smiled, looked out at us and said, "Don didn't really use that word, 'curmudgeon' when talking with me. I used that word as a substitute for what you can probably guess he really said."

WESTERN
HORSEMAN

World's Lead[...] [...]agazine Since 1936

September 1989
$2.25 U.S.
$2.75 Canada

Dick Spencer
1921 — 1989

54TH
YEAR

0   7 4820 08885   09

9

THE "ROARING" '90S

We invested in people.

Dick's passing was a blow to the magazine, or at least to the magazine's staff. The longtime readers were no doubt saddened to learn of his death, but they still expected to receive their magazine each month and weren't disappointed. Fortunately, we had had several months to prepare for an office with no Dick Spencer.

Dick had seen to it that Bill Pennington would be in a position to help run the outfit. His title became general/business manager. Bill knew all about leadership after his long, successful career in the Air Force, and he had plenty of business sense, as well. This was good, because our business manager, Bart Marshall, was retiring. Some of us used to quip that the magazine ran itself, that we really didn't need anyone at the helm because we all did our jobs and everything fell into place automatically month after month. That was faulty thinking, but it took awhile for me to realize it.

Still, it's easy to recall why we were lulled into thinking that way. Dick gave every impression that the business did essentially run itself. Budgets and financial reports bored him. We didn't have budgets; our current budget was whatever we spent the previous year. The truth is, Dick ran *Western Horseman* as per the proverbial "flying by the seat of his pants."

This management style worked beautifully for him. Looking in at Dick, seated at his desk, one was used to seeing him pecking away at his typewriter— or perhaps illustrating a card or doing some type of leather work—rather than poring over business reports. Remember, though, Dick had been tight with money—his own and *Western Horseman's*. This overall conservative approach to life kept the company in good shape. And if someone in the office needed more explanation for the word "no," Dick would give it to him behind a closed door, or perhaps just send him on his way with a joke. I remember a stockholders' meeting when Dick called for the vote of approval on something and then said with a smile, "It doesn't matter whether you like it or not, we're gonna do it anyway."

We took this photo of the WH staff around 1990. There were 30 of us at that time. Bert Anderson, kneeling to the left, put his camera shutter on a timer, and then ran to get in the picture.

Changing With the Times

So, I had the title of publisher, and was made president of the corporation. One of the first things I did was name Pat Close editor—at last. Pat and Corliss already had become members of the board of directors, and Dick was the one who paved the way for this to happen. He suggested at his last stock-holders meeting, shortly before he became ill, that perhaps the board should be expanded with the inclusion of two women (and Pat and Corliss were the obvious candidates). Bill also went on the board of directors, and Chan Bergen and Don Wood continued to serve on the board as well; Don would retire in 1993, leaving Corliss to take over as advertising director. Bart, meanwhile, helped find and train a young man, Herb Barton, who eventually became Bart's replacement. Darrell left the editorial department to start his own publication, *Cowboy* magazine. And we hired a longtime friend of our magazine, Butch Morgan, as marketing director.

At the same time, Dick's widow, Vivian, had a question regarding the value and disposition of Dick's Western Horseman Inc. stock, so one day Pat and I drove downtown to consult with an attorney, Jack Holst, who wound up becoming our company lawyer and mentor on how to run an employee-owned, sub-chapter S corporation with stockholders. Jack became a good friend, and ironically lived on the acreage adjoining Chan and Melitta's property, across the road from the Spencer place, just over the ridge near Scribner's and overlooking the old Flying Horse Ranch. Small world. We settled the Spencer stock litigation in 1991.

Jack explained that Dick had been able to conduct a board or stockholders meeting in such informal fashion because he had been in the position of one who is sharing, and therefore he had the latitude of informality. Early on, Dick could have kept more of the stock for himself and a few close associates; instead he saw that

In the January 1996 issue, our 60th anniversary, we published photos of all our staff members at that time. They're included here again, starting with this photo of Pat and me.

WESTERN HORSEMAN ARCHIVES

Corliss Palmer became advertising director after Don Wood retired.
WESTERN HORSEMAN ARCHIVES

Dwayne Brech, the WH art director, is shown here with his assistant, Jeanne Mazerall.
WESTERN HORSEMAN ARCHIVES

Rick Swan served as the buying guide manager, and Helen Keilers was the advertising assistant in charge of classified ads.
WESTERN HORSEMAN ARCHIVES

the stock for this closed corporation was offered to others in the office as it became available. He helped formulate a process for distributing stock and repurchasing stock when someone left the company, retired or died. When stock was taken back by the corporation, it was purchased according to a formula in a stock purchase agreement signed by each stockholder. Our board liked the idea of offering stock to more employees as it became available, and we continued with this philosophy.

Carol Schutts and Deanna Holt, accounting clerks, helped keep the records straight.
WESTERN HORSEMAN ARCHIVES

Larraine Cocroft, advertising assistant, is shown with Carol Coalson, advertising traffic manager.
WESTERN HORSEMAN ARCHIVES

Kim Simshauser began working for WH *in 1996 and proved to be an invaluable asset in the advertising department.*
JENNIFER DENISON

The graphics department crew included Bert Anderson, production manager, Marilyn Petrenas, typesetting manager, and Glenn Mattingly, graphics assistant.
WESTERN HORSEMAN ARCHIVES

Scott Palmer, Ernie Varoz and Warren Upchurch took care of
shipping and receiving.
WESTERN HORSEMAN ARCHIVES

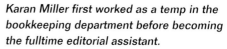

Karan Miller first worked as a temp in the
bookkeeping department before becoming
the fulltime editorial assistant.
JENNIFER DENISON

Advertising Assistants LiAnne Leaveck and Julie
Quinlan completed the department's staffing.
WESTERN HORSEMAN ARCHIVES

Herb Barton, business manager, is shown with Penny Gibson,
assistant business manager.
WESTERN HORSEMAN ARCHIVES

Some called the late Dolores Hickey, our warm and personable receptionist, "The Voice of Western Horseman*" because she was the first one readers talked with when they called or came by the office.*
WESTERN HORSEMAN ARCHIVES

Attention to Detail

Meanwhile, Jack advised, official meetings should be run according to *Robert's Rules of Order.* And that's what we did. I still needed more help in those early days; after all, I had been trained as a journalist, not a businessman. Once again, my old friend and former boss, Chan Bergen, came through for me. He and I chatted one afternoon at his house, where I stopped on my way home from work. What really stuck with me was this piece of advice he offered: "Attention to detail."

Hiring Butch Morgan brought a few laughs back into the office that had been sorely missed since Dick's passing. Butch is a practical joker, quick with the one-liner, a handshake and laugh. When Bill Pennington and I met with Butch at a nearby restaurant, to discuss terms of his employment, we all piled into my rather shabby pickup after lunch. Butch looked at the truck and said, "Apparently a new vehicle isn't part of the deal."

The first week he was employed by us, he and his wife, Charlene, manned a *Western Horseman* booth at a special rodeo in Scottsdale, Arizona. We were one of a variety of sponsors at this event, and Butch's old pal, Hadley Barrett, was working as announcer. Each sponsor got a "plug" from Hadley during opening ceremonies at each performance. I remember, early in the week, Hadley said something kind about *Western Horseman,* sort of along the lines of "... and *Western Horseman* magazine, enjoyed by thousands of readers each month." Next day, Hadley's comments to the crowd were something like "...*Western Horseman,* read by hundreds of thousands around the world." Along about the third performance, the plug was "...*Western Horseman,* read by millions daily!"

I turned to Butch and said, "You haven't worked for us even a week, and already our circulation is going through the roof!"

Part of the reason Butch was hired was to tap into his and Charlene's knack for running a successful promotional booth at horse shows and rodeos. They had honed their skills at this after years of manning the booth for their Blue Ribbon Trophy business, which they eventually sold. Butch knows everyone, remembers names and faces and is always ready to shake hands. Charlene knows how to keep track of the money and inventory, and the result is, to this day, a lot of subscriptions are sold, along with books and calendars, at the *Western Horseman* booth in various horse and rodeo events across the country. I knew the magazine had a few manned booths at several events years earlier, and then the booths had ended, outside of the one at Denver's annual market in January. So, we started in with this and other promotions, and it all seemed to pay off.

There was a national magazine wholesaler convention that happened to be scheduled

at the Broadmoor Hotel, right there in Colorado Springs, that same fall of '89, and several of us attended, including Butch. At the time, *Western Horseman* had a "sell-through" on regular newsstands that averaged 50 percent or better each month. In other words, we sold half of all copies of the magazine placed on all the newsstands. This was a very healthy sell-through, but some of us were so green we didn't realize it at the time. Anyway, the convention hosted magazine publishers, plus the wholesalers (hundreds of companies that actually placed all the magazines on all the newsstands) plus national distributors (the handful of companies that worked on behalf of the magazines to negotiate with wholesalers as to where magazines would be placed on sale and how many copies would be displayed on racks each month). During a coffee break at the convention, Butch set down with one of the other publishers and engaged him in

Butch and Charlene Morgan still represent WH *at equine events throughout the country. My daughter, Mary Claire, and wife, Marsha, stopped by to visit the* WH *booth, which was being manned at the time by Butch, and I shot this picture of the three of them.*
RANDY WITTE

conversation; he asked if the guy had any ideas as to how we could better our sell-through, which was "only 50 percent or so." The fellow told Butch he thought we were doing just fine.

I guess we were, because we found in succeeding years that a good sell-through was getting harder to obtain. In those days, however, we distributed magazines directly to a lot of western wear and feed stores, and the sell-through for them was often an incredible 80 percent. Today's sell-throughs on regular magazine racks in grocery stores and so forth are often less than 40 percent.

The Newsstand

At the convention that year, program speakers told us that the newsstand business was starting to change. In the near future, they said, we would see a chain of "super stores" throughout the country that would stock nearly everything a person would want to buy, like groceries, clothing, hardware, recreational items and also books and magazines. And that these stores would negotiate their own prices for items they wanted to stock. If this news was unsettling to a lot of the conventioneers, you wouldn't have known it.

The system in place for getting magazines into and out of retail stores was somewhat convoluted, but it had worked for decades. A wholesaler supplied all the magazines in any given town or area, and was responsible for receiving bulk magazine deliveries each month, then stocking all the store racks in town, returning to restock any titles that were selling out, and hauling away out-of-date copies for shredding. The retailer kept 20 percent of the cover price of each magazine sold, while 80 percent of the sale went to the wholesaler, who in turn sent 60 percent of the sale to the publisher. The publisher sent around 10 percent of that to the national distributor. Throw into the mix a Retail Display Allowance of perhaps 5 percent, paid by the publisher to the retailer (through the wholesaler) for extra-good placement on a magazine rack, say near the checkout, and you can see how this process could become a little labor intensive. The waste of unsold magazines was (and still is) borne by the publisher, and everyone received checks a couple months later.

The super-store prediction came true most notably with the great expansion of Wal-Mart stores throughout the country during the 1990s. But what really rocked the magazine newsstand distribution business occurred in the mid-90s when the Safeway grocery store chain told wholesalers in several northwestern states that it would no longer do business with hundreds of individual wholesalers city-by-city, but would take bids from wholesalers who offered to supply magazines to all their stores in large regions. Instead of writing hundreds of checks each month to hundreds of wholesale dealers, Safeway wanted to write only a few checks to a few wholesalers. This was viewed as a great idea for retail businesses that offered magazines for sale, and other store chains quickly followed suit.

Wholesalers began buying and selling their companies to one another, and those that were buying got into bidding competition for large chunks of retail business. Successful bidders were those willing to tighten their profit margins—giving more profit to retailers—and as a result everyone else in the magazine business felt the pressure as well. Wholesalers became reluctant to handle any magazines that didn't have a great sell-through, because it cost them money to remove unsold magazines from the racks. Economics also dictated it was no longer profitable for wholesalers to restock most racks more than once a month, and service to a lot of small newsstands in the hinterlands was dropped altogether. None of these things were really conducive for great newsstand sales.

I know, this is Too Much Information, but it was one of the things we wrestled with. Today, incidentally, there are only a handful of wholesalers that rack magazines, and a lot of magazines once available on newsstands are no longer available; many of them went out of business. The 1990s for *Western Horseman*, however, were generally a period of growth. The Audit Bureau of Circulations, which as the name implies provides an official count of total circulation for publications, listed *WH* at 230,322 total newsstand buyers and subscribers as of December 31, 1994. This was just shy of the all-time high of 231,330 set in 1972. Circulation would ebb and flow after that, but the magazine then, and now, continues as a very healthy publication—75 years old and still thriving.

We did a variety of things that decade to promote the magazine and the western industry as a whole. There were special promotions to help boost the number of newsstand buyers and subscribers. We attended various industry conferences and conventions—gatherings in the horse industry as well as the magazine industry. Butch and I even took a *WH* booth to the big Equitana horse show in Essen, Germany, one year, and handed out 15,000 copies of the magazine. We visited with folks from around the world and sold subscriptions. But what we focused on more than anything was maintaining the best editorial staff and producing the best editorial package possible. We invested in people.

A sign hung in the editorial offices that read: "The only way to make a magazine better for the advertiser is to make it better for the reader." That was our creed. Something else that worked to our advantage—reader surveys indicated we had a greater percentage of male readers compared to female readers, while all the other magazines had a leading percentage of female readers. Women, in general, probably spend more on horse items than men, but there were and are some advertisers who have products that appeal mostly to men. With our particular mix of readers, we were pretty much assured of getting those advertisers as well as the others. If anything, we felt we could strengthen the magazine by appealing a little more to women than we had in the past, and still not turn away the men.

More Staff

The spring of 1990, we began expanding the staff, particularly the editorial staff. Pat hired Kathy Kadash as an associate editor. Kathy came to work with a lot of experience as an equine journalist. She had served as editor of *Horseman* magazine in Houston, and prior to that as news editor for *Quarter Horse News* in Fort Worth. She had raised, trained and shown her own Quarter Horses and Paints, participated in competitive trail riding, rode hunters and jumpers and three-gaited horses, as well. Shortly after she was hired, we also hired Kathy's future husband, Rick Swan, who proved to be an all-around hand helping with editorial, advertising and circulation projects. As with most of the staff, Kathy and Rick brought their horses with them.

Fran Smith joined the editorial team initially as a staff writer in 1992. She brought a certain southern flair to the magazine, having been raised at Forrest City, Ark., near Memphis, Tennessee. Her dad was a horseman, and she had grown up showing horses, trail riding and rodeoing; she had competed

In 1996, Gary Vorhes was WH *managing editor, and Kathy Kadash Swan, at left, and Fran Devereux Smith were associate editors for the magazine.*
WESTERN HORSEMAN ARCHIVES

Frank Holmes, a staff writer at the time, is shown with Editorial Assistant Brenda Goodwin.
WESTERN HORSEMAN ARCHIVES

115

Among the perks to a WH *editorial job are all the wonderful people and places you get to visit. Fran Smith participated in a group ride that visited Zion, Bryce, the Arizona Strip Badlands and Grand Canyon for a 1999 article, "The Red Rock Ride." Another rider, Joe Bottoms, took this photo of Fran standing on the edge of the Grand Canyon.*
JOE BOTTOMS

on the Arkansas State University rodeo team and represented her home state in the Miss Rodeo America pageant. Fran also had participated in the Bicentennial Wagon Train Pilgrimage. She had ridden for the public off and on since she was 13, helped 4-H youth and non-pro horsemen, and recently had assisted her husband in a farm and ranch operation on the Red River.

Then, Fran wound up divorced and was looking for a job. She answered a blind ad Pat had placed in *Quarter Horse News:* "Wanted, staff writer for general interest horse magazine."

"When I found out the ad was for *Western Horseman* and Pat was willing to fly me up for an interview, I just knew I had to get that job," Fran recalled. "For people growing up in that part of the country, *Western Horseman* was our window to the stock-horse world. Ernie King (the current *WH* associate publisher who grew up in Mississippi) would say the same thing.

"My mother always said I'd need that college degree some day. I'd never really used it, but there I was, nearly 40 years old, and I think that's what got my foot in the door—the fact I had a broad horse background and a college degree." Eighteen years later, Fran is still working for the magazine. She worked her way up to managing editor, and ramrodded several *WH* books along the way, and today she focuses strictly on book production.

"The first book I was assigned to do, shortly after I got hired, was *First Horse,*" Fran said, "which was supposed to replace those early horsemanship books Dick Spencer had done. Talk about being intimidated, those Dick Spencer books are what I had studied, and to think I was supposed to replace them!"

Fran went on to do other books and booklets, including *Bits and Bitting* with Greg Darnell, which the National Reining Horse Association used as a textbook on bitting for their judging courses. Then came a team roping book with the champions Jake Barnes and Clay O'Brian Cooper, to replace the team roping book I had done with Leo Camarillo. She wrote a book with horseman Curt Pate and is currently finishing a book with multiple world champion Mike Major on ranch-versatility competition.

"To me, that's always been one of the perks of the job," Fran said. "I get to talk to good horsemen, take something home and try it with my own horses. And having the opportunity to see the country, often horseback, is almost as good as talking with those top horsemen."

Fran remembers an in-house survey we did on employees who participated in various horse activities, which was most of the staff. The results pretty much paralleled those of a reader survey we already had done. "The staff and their kids were involved in team roping, horse showing, trail riding, you name it. Carol Coalson (in advertising) had a daughter, Jenny, who won the Little Britches all-around; Helen Keilers (also in advertising) had a son roping on a college rodeo team; Penny Gibson (who worked in accounting) was winning at the Paint Horse shows; Mary Claire (Witte) and Christy (Morgan) were winning at the Quarter Horse shows; Amy and Tara (Vorhes) were playing collegiate polo, and Gary was playing polo, too. Butch and his entire family were roping .... We were our readership. We really were producing a magazine for ourselves."

Pat continued to round out the editorial staff in 1994 by hiring horse historian Frank Holmes as a staff writer. Frank brought with him a good 30 years of horse experience, and had written for various magazines including *WH*. He's one of those persons with a memory for pedigrees, especially Appaloosas, Quarter Horses, Paints and Palominos. He had met and written about a lot of the legendary breeders through the years, and continued this practice for the *WH* line of *Legends* books. Among his best contributions was *The Hank Wiescamp Story*, biography of the legendary Colorado horseman, and later, on his own, *Wire to Wire*, the story of Walter Merrick, renowned Quarter Horse and racehorse man.

In 1998, A.J. Mangum joined the *WH* editorial department as an associate editor. And his future wife, Roy Jo Sartin, also came to work in the magazine's editorial department

A. J. Mangum had experience with two breed publications, The *Quarter Horse Journal* and *Appaloosa Journal, before coming to* WH.
AJ MANGUM

shortly thereafter. A.J. had worked at *The Quarter Horse Journal*, where he was a writer and field editor, and prior to that he was editor-in-chief at the *Appaloosa Journal*. He was raised on a central-Oregon horse and cattle ranch, and was graduated from Oregon State University with a degree in management and a minor in journalism. A.J. would be a future editor of *Western Horseman*.

Finally, Pat arranged in 1999 to hire Juli Thorson as contributing editor, working from her home in Moscow, Idaho. Juli grew up with horses and reading *Western Horseman* in North Dakota. She had a broad background riding and showing horses, and had graduated with a journalism degree from the University of North Dakota. She went on to become a distinguished equine journalist, working for *Appaloosa News, The Lariat* (a horsemen's newspaper in Oregon), *California Horse*

Review, Performance Horseman, and *Horse & Rider.* At *Western Horseman* she wrote feature articles with top trainers, plus a column, "Personally Speaking."

Incidentally, out of all the columns written through the years, Baxter Black's syndicated "On the Edge of Common Sense" continues to be the most popular with readers. Many of those columns now have been compiled in a *WH* book, *The Back Page.*

A Few Laughs

Butch Morgan, as I said earlier, helped bring some laughs to the office after Dick's passing. He was, as Gary Vorhes always said, "an impractical joker," and really delighted in pulling pranks on people, mostly harmless and often on Gary, who sometimes retaliated. There was the time Gary, Butch and I had lunch in a restaurant, Gary went off to the restroom before we all returned to work—and left his hat on the seat right next to Butch. Without even pausing, Butch picked up a paper napkin, folded it over and placed it inside the hatband. I guess we both thought Gary would feel the difference immediately

and we would all have a laugh. But Gary wore the hat without a word and we all returned to the office, completely forgetting the "hat trick."

Three days later, Gary walked through the front door and complained about his hat. He happened to be standing outside Butch's office, and Butch watched him take his hat off and begin to examine the inside of it. A big red spot was visible on Gary's forehead. Gary looked at Butch and knew—immediately— the cause of his discomfort.

He also knew whom to blame the time he picked up his phone and the earpiece coated his ear with Vaseline.

Then there was the time Gary had his saddle shipped to him from a trip he had taken. A big box arrived at the office, containing the saddle, and after retrieving his saddle, Gary looked at the box and got an idea. Butch was gone right then, so Gary simply turned the box upside down in the middle of Butch's office. Butch knew his recent actions were overdue for retaliation of some kind, and when he eyed the box, he turned to Dolores Hickey, our receptionist,

Marsha and I raised a few foals through the years. This one, unfortunately, was an orphan. I snapped this picture of my wife giving the little guy a bottle, then wrote a "Leading Off" column about it. Readers responded with advice. The colt wound up in good hands and made a nice team roping horse.

RANDY WITTE

Mike Laughlin and Gary Vorhes were photographed horseback in 2008 on the Maggie Creek Cattle Company, Lamoille Division, at Lamoille, Nev., where Mike has buckarooed in recent years. Mike is a top cowboy and has worked on ranches throughout the West, and he is a longtime WH contributor. His partner and soul mate, Lee Raine, a true lady of the West, is the excellent photographer who took this shot. Gary and Mike were checking outside cattle and had Mike's cow dogs, Tip and Taz, with them. Mike's horse is a Colonel Pic-bred, 6-year-old snaffle-bit horse from California, and Gary is riding Mike's other horse, a gelding out of a Young Bert stallion, raised by the Van Norman family and started by Mike's son, Pat.

LEE RAINE

and asked about it. Dolores played ignorant and Butch would not go close to the box—for the next three days!

Gary's stroke of genius with Butch was the time Gary took a long-playing tape from a particular country-western singer Butch didn't care for, and set it to playing—very faintly—in one of Butch's desk drawers.

Butch is a little hard of hearing anyway, so he had trouble locating the source of this soft singing that was slowly driving him crazy. He walked out of his office and asked Dolores if she could hear it. Dolores was in on the joke, of course, and said no. An hour or so later, Butch was back in Gary's office, making accusations.

In the 1990s I became active with our local Pikes Peak or Bust Rodeo and was proud to serve on the board, and honored to be president by the end of the decade. The great rodeo photographer Louise Serpa took this picture of me during the grand entry in 2000.

LOUISE SERPA

There was a trail outside the office, and some of the women used it to go for walks on breaks. To get to the trail, they had to walk by whatever vehicles were parked out front. That's when Butch would pull out his truck keys and hit the button to honk the horn and flash the lights, startling the hikers.

Butch wanted his own computer for a long time, and we never seemed to get around to buying it for him. Finally, though, we did order a computer for Butch, and told him it was on the way. That same week, Pat ran across a toy computer at K-Mart, down the street. She and a handful of other

staffers chipped in to buy the toy and have it "installed" at Butch's desk while he was in the coffee room. It was a good joke, and Butch got as much fun out of the joke as anyone.

Pat continued working through 2001—40 years at the magazine—and considers it a "wonderful career for someone who started at the magazine as a horse-crazy young girl. It was a great vocation and avocation, and I loved it. There were bumps along the way, and one time I even thought about looking for another job, but I thought I liked what I was doing, so I'll just stay put, and it all worked out. It ended beautifully. I never thought I'd be editor.

"The magazine was so well-respected and so well-liked that anyone on the staff was always welcome to get interviews with trainers, breeders and ranchers, and we always had to remember that we were not welcomed because of who we were, but because of who we represented." That realization still holds true today.

Gary Vorhes, also now retired, echoed similar sentiments: "Wherever we went on assignment, people seemed gracious, but I always remembered, they weren't necessarily so nice because I was such a great person, but because I worked for *Western Horseman.* Something else we figured out—we were going places and seeing things that the readers really would have liked to have gone and seen themselves. We were doing it for the readers. Every issue of the magazine was a little window to the West for a lot of people who couldn't be there themselves.

"I also felt we always tried to have articles in each issue that would provide something for just about everyone. That we were giving the readers a little present every month; it's true they were paying us to do that. But when you got the issue and flipped through the ranch, training, veterinary, vacation trips articles, you'd like to think they were going to be very happy to get that issue. I always thought that was a big part of the satisfaction of our magazine, because it was—and still is—the best damn horse magazine there is!

"In my humble estimation."

So there you have it—a collection of historical facts and recollections from others and myself who played roles in The World's Leading Horse Magazine, since 1936. The *Western Horseman,* as I said at the outset, provided a wonderful career for me and my family. Today, Marsha and I raise Longhorn cattle in the northern part of the county, about 25 miles from the old *WH* office. We still have horses, and our daughter, Mary Claire, son-in-law Trey Niemeyer, and grandson Time, live on the place next to ours. The years have gone by all too quickly, and a nearly new staff is in place at the magazine. But for so many of us who worked at the magazine in the past, it will always be with us. I still receive the magazine in the mail each month, and can't help but look for it as I walk past a newsstand. If I spot the *Western Horseman* on a shelf, I always pause to straighten up the copies, and make sure no other titles are covering it up.

I'm not the only one who does this.

Toward the end of the 1990s, our business manager, Herb Barton, started eyeing and analyzing retirement dates for our major stockholders. He and the rest of the board gradually realized a lot of stock would have to be brought back into the corporation in the near future and in a relatively short time frame. The magazine was doing great, but we didn't wish to possibly jeopardize its future with our commitment to purchase stock from retirees. The stock valuation had continued to increase, year after year. Finally, a decision was made to sell to a much larger media company, and on September 1, 2001, Morris Communications Company became the new owner of *Western Horseman* magazine. A new chapter was beginning.

This George Phippen art was used on a commemorative buckle celebrating the magazine's 60th anniversary in 1996.

10

Into the 21st Century

How things have changed!

A span of 75 years is a blink of the eye in world history, but to most of us, seven-and-a-half decades seem like a lengthy passage of time. For a magazine to be in continuous publication that long is worthy of celebration and says a lot about *Western Horseman's* staff, its readers and, of course, the subject itself.

A shared interest in horses always has bonded readers and writers of *Western Horseman,* and though the magazine continues to evolve in the way it looks and is produced, this interest (some would say passion) is probably the one "constant." Certainly, the nature of the magazine's staff hasn't changed much. I look at the staff today and can easily picture them working for the magazine decades ago, and the reverse is also true. Those staff members of bygone years probably could have been at home in the modern *Western Horseman.*

But how things have changed! Remember reading about Paul and Worth Albert working at night by kerosene lantern to get the first issue out? The Alberts would have to be amazed at the way this publication comes together today. I know I am

amazed at the changes in production that have come about just over the last decade. For one thing, the magazine is still printed on paper, but that's about the only use of paper in the entire process. Today, everything is assembled and produced electronically. Typewriters went by the wayside years ago, with the introduction of computers, but now all photographs are taken with digital cameras. Articles and photographs are assembled and edited on computer screens, rather than pasted up on dummy boards. Gone are the days when camera-ready copy or page negatives were shipped to the printer. Today, the printing plant receives everything it needs to print the next issue of *Western Horseman* when the magazine's production department sends the material via the Internet.

The magazine shows up reliably each month in the subscriber's mailbox and also is available on the newsstand, but that's not all. Today, readers can visit the *Western Horseman* Web site at westernhorseman.com and learn about upcoming articles, read related features onscreen, learn what it's like to gather ranch stories and training features by reading

Billy Morris is riding to a win in the Augusta Futurity.

THE *AUGUSTA CHRONICLE* STAFF

staff-written blogs. Readers can join Club *Western Horseman* and receive special services and additional information. They can communicate with other readers and voice opinions on the magazine and its content. Books, DVDs and audios are readily available online, too. Advertisers provide easy online access to a wide range of products, and there is direct access to Horsecity.com, the all-inclusive equine site that is also owned by *Western Horseman's* parent company, Morris Communications Co. LLC.

William S. "Billy" Morris III

Yes, *WH* is part of a well-respected, midsize media company that operates across the United States and abroad, and the magazine leads a fleet of equine publications owned by the company. In addition to *Western Horseman,* the company also owns *Quarter Horse News* (purchased in 1981), *Barrel Horse News* (which they started in 1996), the *Horsemen's Yankee Pedlar* (purchased in 2001), and *Horsecity .com,* an online entity established in 2000. William S. "Billy" Morris III is CEO and chairman of Morris Communications, and is the man responsible for creating an equine branch of publishing within the company. This endeavor came to fruition, no doubt, due to an ongoing case of "equine fever," a malady he contracted as a youth. "There is no known cure for equine fever," he says, "but the symptoms can be treated. You simply get a good horse, a saddle, and go riding. And that gives immediate relief."

Billy's earliest memory of horses was when he was an infant being held in his grandfather's arms, riding down a road to his grandfather's farm in Aiken, South

Augusta Futurity Show Manager Pete May, at left, William S. "Billy" Morris, and now-retired National Cutting Horse Association Executive Director Zack T. Wood displayed championship buckles for the 1999 Georgia event.
THE *AUGUSTA CHRONICLE* STAFF

This Morris family portrait was taken in autumn 2009. At left, dressed in blue, is Susie Morris Baker with her husband, Dr. Lee Baker, and their four children (from left) Lee Jr., Mary Ellis, Alden, and Ben. Billy and Sissie Morris are in the center. To the right, dressed in red, are Caroline and Will Morris with their sons Gray (at left) and William. Tyler Morris is at the far right. The three Morris children are Susie, Will (William S. Morris IV), and Tyler.

MARK ALBERTIN

Carolina. As a child, Billy took riding lessons in his home town of Augusta, Ga., where his father, William S. Morris II, was running the family newspaper business—the local *Augusta Chronicle* and *Augusta Herald*. Billy was about 10 years old, during World War II, when his father gave him his own horse. The 14-hand part-Hackney was known as Baron.

"I never realized it at the time," Billy recalled, "but my father was trying to teach some important lessons of life by giving me Baron. I know now that my father was very wise. He realized that my owning a horse was a great opportunity to teach a young boy some valuable lessons: responsibility, accountability and the proper care of animals." A stable and paddock were built in the backyard, where Baron and his stable

mate, a goat named Billy-Billy, lived, and it was shortly thereafter that Baron and Billy Morris both went to work for the family business, delivering newspapers horseback around town each morning.

The two traveled through the neighborhood, and Billy would fling papers in the direction of front porches, and Baron would pause and brace against each throw. The goat followed along behind for company initially, but soon was relieved of that duty when neighbors complained about him eating the flowers out of their yards.

"So, early in my life," Billy said, "my little horse taught me to be responsible for my property; to be accountable for my acts; to serve my customers with care and sensitivity; and that it is all right to mix business and pleasure and to make a profit doing it."

Billy outgrew his role of newspaper boy and eventually graduated with a B.A. degree in journalism from the University of Georgia. A few days before his 22nd birthday in 1956, he became assistant to the president in the family business. Ten years later he became publisher of the two Augusta newspapers and president of the corporation. As years went by he became a leader in the media industry, serving as president of the Newspaper Association of America, past member of Associated Press board of directors and the Advertising Council Inc. He received the first Bottom Line Award from the Media Management Club of the University of Georgia for his contributions to publications management education at the school, and in 1983 he was named Outstanding Alumnus of the school's Grady College of Journalism and Mass Communication.

Because Billy always has been a strong supporter for various community projects in towns and cities served by Morris Communications, those communities have said thank you to him. For example, he is an inductee in the Mass Communication Hall of Fame at Lubbock's Texas Tech University School of Communications, and, of course, the Lubbock *Avalanche Journal,* incidentally,

is a longtime Morris Communications publication. In Lubbock he also was presented with the American Cowboy Culture Award for Western Writing and Publishing, an honor that also has been bestowed on Dick Spencer and me in other years. In his hometown, Billy received the Greater Augusta Arts Council President's Award for initiating a study that led to creation of a cultural arts corridor to revitalize Augusta's riverfront.

These and other accolades have come to Billy Morris throughout his career, but he says his proudest accomplishment was persuading Mary Sue "Sissie" Ellis of Columbus, Ga., to become his wife. Billy and Sissie have been married for 52 years. They have two sons, Will and Tyler, a daughter, Susie Baker, and six grandchildren.

Through the years, Billy's interest in horses has never waned. By the 1970s, he and Sissie owned a farm in South Carolina, where they had Quarter Horses and cattle. By the mid-1970s he had been introduced to the sport of cutting, and became "hooked" on riding cutting horses. One thing led to another, and he became instrumental in bringing the first major cutting horse contest to the Southeast—the Augusta Cutting Horse Futurity. Billy became show chairman,

Billy Morris is driving the Western Horseman *stagecoach in a parade.*
THE *AUGUSTA CHRONICLE* STAFF

Billy Morris is riding here with grandsons Lee Baker Jr. and Ben Baker.
COURTESY THE MORRIS FAMILY

and the futurity has thrived as a major event in the National Cutting Horse Association for more than 33 years. Each January, the Augusta Futurity attracts some 30,000 spectators, as well as the top cutting-horse trainers and riders from around the country. Billy not only has supervised this event, he has competed and won in it, as well.

Morris Communications

When Morris Communications bought *Quarter Horse News* in 1981, it was a small Texas racing weekly. Billy changed the focus to western performance events, including cutting, reining, roping and barrel racing, and made it semimonthly. Then he developed Equi-Stat, a database that tracks money earned in western performance events and links these totals to pedigrees, something that had never been done. In a similar vein, he began a *Performance Horse Sales Price Guide,* filled with data on horses sold with proof of transfer to new owners. Included are overall sales analysis, rankings of sires and dams, and examples of good crosses based on performance-event earnings.

In 1994, Billy launched the National Barrel Horse Association, which features a division classification format that has had a dramatic impact on the growth of barrel racing. These endeavors, plus the acquisition of other equine publications, including the crown jewel, *Western Horseman,* led Billy Morris to the University of Louisville in 2002, where he received the 13th annual John W. Galbreath Award for Outstanding Entrepreneurship in the Equine Industry.

During his acceptance speech for the Galbreath Award, which was made to an audience filled with university students, Billy shared some of the lessons he has learned in business, and in the business of life itself. A portion of his remarks bear repeating here. They provide sound advice and offer insight into the way Billy Morris conducts his life.

"1. Your attitude is your biggest asset," he said. "How you think is everything. Your glass must always be half-full. Think success, not failure. Be positive. Be aware of negative environments and avoid them. Someone once told me, 'Attitude is the paintbrush you color your

127

life with.' Think about that! That's a pretty good expression. I like that and I agree with it.

"2. Be friendly. Be likable. Deal and communicate with people fairly, honestly and effectively.

"3. Be honest. Above all, be honest with yourself, as well as with others. Your word must be your bond. Take responsibility for what you do and be dependable. If people know they can count on you, they will respect you and want to deal with you.

"4. Decide what you want to be. What are your goals? Write them down on a piece of paper. Be specific. Put them in 5-, 10- and 20-year brackets. Then, develop a plan, a written plan, on how you will accomplish these goals. Be sure they are clear, and then go after them. Be persistent and work hard. Never give up….

"5. Get help. Lots of folks will help young people along the way, especially if they like them and particularly if they have similar interests….

"6. After your plan takes shape, then take action. Goals are nothing unless you act to make them happen and be persistent. Someone said, 'Success is a marathon, not a sprint.' I believe that.

"7. Never stop learning. When you get out of college with a degree… don't think your learning and studying are over. They are not. Actually, they have just begun. The world in which we live is changing every day, and you and I must change with it….

"8. Finally, I would recommend that you stay focused. Don't be distracted. Focus your time, energy and money on your goals, and it will pay off for you."

The first Western Horseman *Award in 2005 recognized Ray Hunt as the embodiment of the values the magazine most respects— Western horsemanship, education, authenticity, ethics and a passion for the Western way of life.*
WESTERN HORSEMAN ARCHIVES

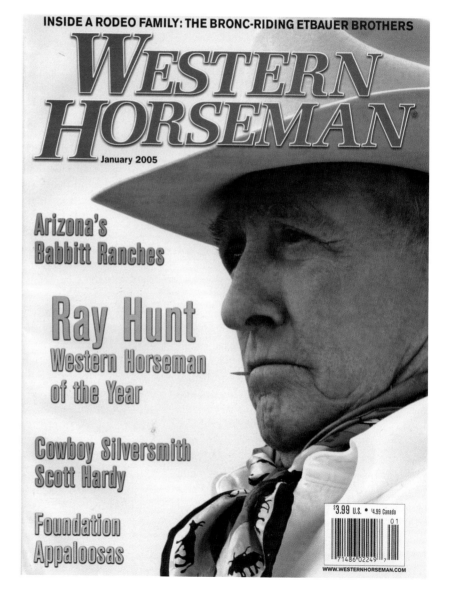

INSIDE A RODEO FAMILY: THE BRONC-RIDING ETBAUER BROTHERS

WESTERN HORSEMAN

January 2005

Arizona's Babbitt Ranches

Ray Hunt
Western Horseman of the Year

Cowboy Silversmith Scott Hardy

Foundation Appaloosas

$3.99 U.S. • $4.99 Canada

WWW.WESTERNHORSEMAN.COM

Billy is a lifelong Christian who said his faith "has been my rock. It has provided me with answers to some of the most fundamental questions of life and has given me the principles on which to live my life."

He is also a strong proponent of freedom of the press, which is no surprise, and he adds that without freedom of the press, there is no freedom. He believes in the free-enterprise system, with a minimum of government involvement. "The role of government," he said, "is to free the American spirit, not to shackle it, to create conditions under which the free-enterprise system will flourish, not wither. Therefore, the less government in business, the better."

As for horses, Billy quipped, "I really don't know why I love horses so. The truth is that I should hate them. They have kicked me, bitten me, bucked me off, tried to run away with me, taken my money, broken my heart, disappointed me and stepped on my toes. But despite all of that, I love them."

Along with the announcement of new ownership to our *WH* readers in the October 2001 issue, I quoted Billy as saying, "Our love of horses has been for pleasure, use on the plantation, and competition. They have given us much enjoyment (and) we are committed to serving the needs of the equine community that raises, trains, rides, buys, and sells." Billy Morris welcomed readers to his company and assured them that "we are committed to strong journalistic ethics and will carry on the stellar traditions and principles of the premier magazine in the equine world."

This has happened, and the magazine continues to offer a variety of articles and photographs that meet the needs of contemporary horsemen and women who like a combination of useful information and entertainment each month. Overseeing the operation is the man who took over as publisher when I retired in 2006, Darrell Dodds.

Darrell Dodds

Life is filled with small incidents that sometimes lead to major outcomes. That's how Darrell Dodds began a journey that put him in key positions within the horse industry, and ultimately into the publisher's chair for *Western Horseman.*

He was raised on the family dairy operation in California's San Joaquin Valley, where his dad kept a few horses to move cattle around to various lots and pastures. One

WH *Publisher Darrell Dodds is shown horseback at his home near Krum, Texas.*
COURTESY DARRELL DODDS

evening, some folks showed up at the front door and asked if the Dodds family would be interested in joining a saddle club they were starting. They had noticed a couple horses out front. Darrell was 5 or 6 years old at the time, and remembers how his father promptly joined the new club.

"My dad always liked horses and he really took to all the games, mostly gymkhana events, this club started doing," Darrell recalled. "They organized parade rides, and it seems like we went to a parade most every weekend during the summers for awhile. A few years later the club put in some roping chutes, so we started doing a little breakaway roping. I was never very good at it but my brother, Al, went on to become a pretty good calf roper.

"So, it's funny how a couple people show up at your door, invite you to a little saddle club meeting, and next thing you know it's pretty much what the whole family recreation is built around."

Not to mention vocations. Al Dodds went on to rope professionally and train Quarter Horses and Thoroughbreds. And Darrell got into the horse industry by way of a journalism career after graduating from San Jose State University. He gained experience as a newspaper reporter, then started his own paper, a weekly called the *Green Mountain Gazette,* in Quincy, California. A friend, Bill Sheppard, was business manager of the paper for awhile, then departed to work for the *California Horse Review.* Eventually, Bill went to the *Paint Horse Journal.*

"Bill called me one day and said he heard the Appaloosa Horse Club was looking for an editor, and wondered if I'd be interested," Darrell recalled, then added. "I was interested, so I made a phone call, interviewed with them, found someone who was interested in taking over the paper, and I moved to Moscow, Idaho, in 1982."

Darrell was there for 10 years. He put out the *Appaloosa News* (which later became the *Appaloosa Journal*), and it was during this tenure Darrell made the most import "hire" of his career. Marty Newman answered an ad he had placed for a production manager. Darrell not only hired Marty for the position, he wound up marrying her in 1987. Darrell went on to serve as executive secretary of the Appaloosa Horse Club from 1988 till 1992. That's when Ed Roberts, executive secretary of the American Paint Horse Association, phoned Darrell and asked if he would be willing to move to Fort Worth, Texas, and take over the *Paint Horse Journal*—Bill Sheppard was retiring as editor.

"There was no master plan to my career," Darrell said. "It was just a series of opportunities that fed off of previous experience. And I happened to land at the Paint Horse Association at the ideal time—the breed was just starting to get some momentum. When I started doing the *Journal* they had around 11,000 subscribers, and when I left 10 years later they had 37,000 and the association had more than 100,000 members. It was booming!

I left in 2002 to be editor of *Horse and Rider* magazine, and was there until 2006, when I came over to *Western Horseman.*"

Darrell is candid about his views of *Western Horseman* in the "new media" age.

"We just can't rely on print alone any longer," he said. "We also have changing demographics. Our core reader is still an adult male and probably in his 40s or 50s, who has experience with horses and has an affinity for western stock-type horses and the lifestyle that is associated with it—everything from movies to music to literature, food, art. But I think we've seen a cultural shift. Fewer of our readers are ranch-raised. More of them probably own a business in town and still like cowboying on the weekends, but they don't have the same connection to the land that readers of 15, 20 or 40 years ago had. Consequently, the nature of the magazine has changed some degree and will continue evolving.

"The challenge we have is to stay true to our core reader and yet be innovative, creative and contemporary enough to be of interest to a 25- or 30-year-old. The way we reach those people isn't just through the newsstand. It's on Facebook, using social media; a lot of them want to know what's in the magazine before the paper copy even shows up. As a result, we must have a technologically savvy staff that understands and knows how to use this media. We also have to continue to look for ways to add to the base of readers—and the advertisers are pushing this even faster than we are. They want to know who the readers are, where they live, what their interests are in horses and other things. Everyone in media today is dealing with the same thing; we aren't unique.

"But the really nice thing about *Western Horseman* is our readers are still very loyal. They love the publication and have supported the changes we've introduced the last few years, giving it a fresh face and a little more emphasis on photography. We still get fan letters and phone calls, and when we go to a trade show or whatever, people find out we're with *WH* and they're more than eager to tell us what they like about the magazine, how much it means to them. As long as we can continue a relationship like that with our readers, we'll be okay.

"I don't think we have a person on the staff who doesn't own a horse, and who doesn't ride at every opportunity. It's not something we do because it's a job; we all love horses and the culture around them. We're horse people and we like other horse people."

Ernie King

Associate Publisher Ernie King is one of those unique individuals who has pretty much "done it all" in the horse world. It's entirely accurate to say he brings an all-around perspective to his job at the magazine.

Ernie grew up in central Mississippi, near a little town named Clinton. His grandfather raised cattle, so he was exposed to that side of the rural lifestyle, but Ernie's dad was really interested in horses, especially Appaloosas. The family had a 120-acre farm with lighted arena and barns where they boarded as many as 80 horses.

"We put on amateur horse shows," Ernie said. "Mom ran the concession stand, Dad was the announcer, and the kids would all work. And then we wound up putting on some 'buck-outs.' We got an El Torro bucking machine, installed some chutes and bought eight practice bulls. My brothers and friends would get on them. I ended up working for some amateur stock contractors, flanking bulls, working around the chutes."

His father also had a combination feed store, western store and saddle shop, where Ernie and his brother worked a spell, making rodeo chaps, bareback riggings and other leather goods, and repairing saddles, too.

In 1990, Ernie went to work for himself, making a living with his own stallions and mares until he wound up going to work for Morris Communications as an advertising sales representative. In January 2002 he joined *Western Horseman,* where he continued as a sales rep and also helped with the *WH* booth at the various trade shows and horse events around the country. He worked his way up in the company to general manager and eventually to associate publisher.

But Ernie has to laugh at himself. "It's ironic," he says. "I ended up in this position because of my lifelong experience with horses. And now I find myself sitting in front of a computer all day. You hear a lot about people wanting things on their ipods and so forth, but I believe the kind of people who are attracted to *WH* mostly are going to be attracted to a print magazine. To begin with, they would rather be horseback than in front of a computer screen. Sometimes the experts want to compare our readership to other mainstream magazine readers, but I don't really think you can do that. They're cut from a different cloth.

"Still, we interact with people in a variety of ways. The magazine itself is always going to be the main focus, but we have readers in other places, too, like Facebook—we have 30,000 *WH* fans on Facebook. And Cory Wiese, our digital media manager, will post things on Facebook several times a week, maybe write a blog, and people will respond with comments and then go to our Web site for more information or to read a complete article.

"Jennifer Denison, our senior editor, is like the Queen of Facebook for us," Ernie continued. "She writes a lot, every day, and the readers enjoy her."

Jennifer is a veteran *WH* staffer who joined the magazine in 2002. She graduated

Ernie King's varied background in the horse industry serves him well in his position as associate publisher for WH.
GRANT HEID

131

Much of Mitch Miller's sales career has been focused on the equine industry.
COURTESY MITCH MILLER

Charlene and Butch Morgan continue to attend trade shows at major events on behalf of the outfit.
COURTESY THE MORGAN FAMILY

Ron Bonge is WH's award-winning art director.
COURTESY RON BONGE

Sales representative Sanders Lawson is holding "Skip" while "Sophie" grazes at Lawson's Kentucky home.
COURTESY SANDY LAWSON

Advertising sales rep Jenn Sanders competed in the sponsors' cutting at the National Cutting Horse Association's Summer Spectacular in Fort Worth.
DON SHUGART

Rayanne Engel-Currin, shown here at the Sharon Camarillo Classic in Reno, Nev., is the senior account manager for the WH sales department.
PROSPORTSPIX

This shot of Cory Wiese, WH's digital media manager, was taken at the Indio, Calif., Professional Rodeo Cowboys Association rodeo.

GENE HYDER PHOTOS

Kami Peterson, a WH *sales rep who lives in Colorado, often team ropes with her son, Shane.*

LISA DICKENS

AJ Mangum packed a camera even when he worked horseback to pursue a feature article.

COURTESY AJ MANGUM

Bobbie Cook, a WH advertising sales representative, is shown here with her 14-year-old Quarter Horse mare, Haileys Comet 496.

COURTESY BOBBIE COOK

During a road trip, Fran Smith's pack trip through South Dakota's Black Hills ended in the Old West town of Deadwood.

COURTESY FRAN D. SMITH

Jennifer Denison lives the western lifestyle and loves to write about it.
DARLENE RUTH

He was born in Texas and grew up there, mostly. His father was in the U.S. Air Force and the family moved around a bit, but wherever they lived, they had horses. Dad was passionate about raising halter horses, and Ross remembers riding along on a lot of cross-country trips, hauling mares to stallions.

Ross went to college at Texas A&M, and that's when he really learned to ride. "I took nine hours of equine science, including basic horsemanship," Ross said. "I signed up for a colt-starting class and just loved it. There were some Ray Hunt principles they were using at that point, so I got introduced to those concepts about making the right things easy. When I got out of college I got a job with the *Paint Horse Journal,* plus my dad had a couple older mares that had never been broke to ride, so I started training them to go under saddle. Since then, I've continued to start one or two horses a year."

Ross also credits the years he has spent interviewing top horsemen in cutting, reining and roping, and using their principles to help with his own horsemanship and training projects. He has a 5-year-old bay mare he raised and trained, Small Town Fritzi by Bueno Fritzi Nick, a finalist in the National Reining Horse Association futurity in 1996.

"What I like about her is she's out of a mare my dad raised and she's a granddaughter on the bottom side of the first horse my dad ever bought."

Ross has enjoyed taking his mare to some ranches and brandings, and is showing her at ranch-versatility events. "We haven't won yet, but we certainly go in there and compete and have fun with it," he said.

Ross' major in college was English and he minored in journalism. Darrell Dodds is the man who hired Ross, fresh out of college, to work at the *Paint Horse Journal* as an assistant editor. "Darrell taught me a lot about photography and magazines, and Dan Streeter, a copy editor there, was a very good coach when it came to writing. Frank Holmes was there at the time, and he taught me a lot about the history of horses and really helped me understand the horse business better than I had before that."

After five years, Ross went to the *Cuttin' Horse Chatter,* where he got to know a lot about the cutting-horse industry. And two years later he was at *Performance Horse,*

from Colorado State University with two bachelor's degrees, one in technical journalism and the other in equine science—a perfect combination! Jennifer has specialized in writing about horses, training and the western lifestyle for the past 15 years. She works from home in Woodland Park, Colo., a mountain community west of Colorado Springs, and loves to help neighboring ranchers, especially at brandings.

Ross Hecox

The current *WH* editor is Ross Hecox, who took on this position in July 2010. That's when 8-year veteran editor A.J. Mangum assumed the position of editor-at-large, working from his home east of Colorado Springs. Ross is based at *WH* headquarters in Fort Worth, Texas.

Editor Ross Hecox is shown with his mare, Small Town Fritzi.
COURTESY ROSS HECOX

where he stayed for two years before hiring on at *WH* in the fall of 2006.

Today, his job involves a variety of tasks, everything from managing a staff to planning issues of the magazine. He credits every successful issue to a "team effort," praises the valuable contributions of freelance writers, and looks forward to contributing more training and ranching articles himself. Ross continues to ride as much as possible when he's home, to stay in good physical condition as much as anything.

"We go to a lot of ranches and spend time riding with them. There have been times I helped out with whatever operation they were working on, whether it was riding and gathering cattle or flanking calves. Not that I'm an expert at these things, but sometimes if a guy experiences things firsthand it helps him to be a better writer."

Ross remembers when he picked up his first copy of *Western Horseman*. It was the April 1988 issue, and he got it at a Love's truck stop in Oklahoma City. He was 13 years old, driving with his dad, who was hauling some mares to a stud farm, and they had stopped for gas and something to snack on. "I saw that cover and it just grabbed me," Ross said. "I bought it off the newsstand and became a subscriber after that. And it wasn't long after I was published in *Western Horseman* for the first time. I did a drawing of a horse, saddled and ground-tied, and sent it to the magazine. It was published in the 'Young Horseman' section."

So, thanks to a truck-stop newsstand in Oklahoma City, we gained a new reader, a contributor to the magazine and a future editor. That's pretty much the way things work around *Western Horseman.*

APPENDIX

Editor's note: In this 1976 reprint, Dick Spencer reflects on four decades of change in the horse industry.

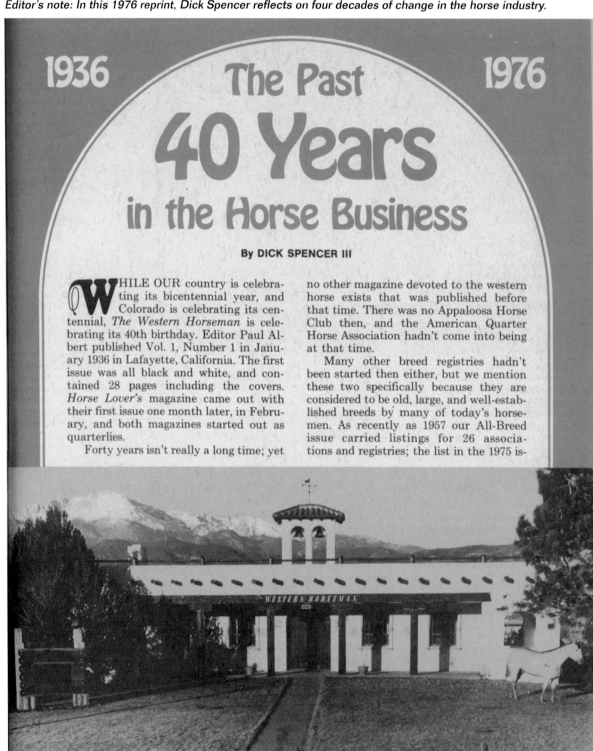

1936 1976

The Past
40 Years
in the Horse Business

By DICK SPENCER III

WHILE OUR country is celebrating its bicentennial year, and Colorado is celebrating its centennial, *The Western Horseman* is celebrating its 40th birthday. Editor Paul Albert published Vol. 1, Number 1 in January 1936 in Lafayette, California. The first issue was all black and white, and contained 28 pages including the covers. *Horse Lover's* magazine came out with their first issue one month later, in February, and both magazines started out as quarterlies.

Forty years isn't really a long time; yet no other magazine devoted to the western horse exists that was published before that time. There was no Appaloosa Horse Club then, and the American Quarter Horse Association hadn't come into being at that time.

Many other breed registries hadn't been started then either, but we mention these two specifically because they are considered to be old, large, and well-established breeds by many of today's horsemen. As recently as 1957 our All-Breed issue carried listings for 26 associations and registries; the list in the 1975 is-

138

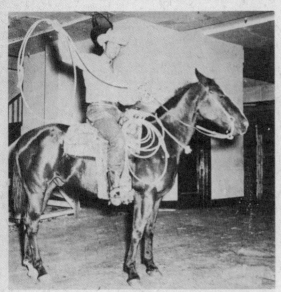

• Jake McClure was a great roper and rodeo hand in his day, and is now memorialized in the Cowboy Hall of Fame.

• Clyde Burk on Baldy, an all-time great rope horse. Note the foreleg scars as a result of a trailer fire. John Stryker Photo

sue carried 67 associations!

A fact that some people might have forgotten, too, is that back in those days this country thought the horse was headed for the path of the dodo bird. Each year the Department of Agriculture put out another bulletin telling how many fewer horses there were than the previous year.

We are not trying to take credit for the recent surge of horse interest, because it was very likely a combination of several things. It got off to a shaky start, and then came World War II to stir our country into an upheaval. With its ending, however, the comparative prosperity with more leisure time and more money, coupled with the

surge towards recreation, all contributed. We reported, helped where we could, and grew right along with the renewed interest in western horses and western riding.

History? Forty years? Admittedly, history is boring to some people, and to old-timers forty years doesn't sound like much history. But let's do some delving into the recent past, and see just what forty years has meant to the history of the western horse. Many of you have been pioneers and haven't realized it.

Let's take rodeo first. Sure, it goes way back. And there are already arguments as to where it started, when it started, and how it started. We've reported those

theories and arguments, and won't go into them again right now. But we know that in June 1847 there was a "contest for roping and throwing" held in Santa Fe, New Mexico. And in 1869 an Englishman named Emilnie Gardenshire was proclaimed "Champion Bronco Buster of the Plains" in a contest between the Campstool, Hashknife, and Mill Iron outfits on the grassy flats near Deer Trail, Colorado. On July 4, 1883, they roped longhorns on the main street of Pecos, Tex.; and in 1888 the citizens of Prescott, Ariz., fenced some land and charged admission for the "first paid-admission rodeo."

Cheyenne Frontier Days, the

• Pete Grubb made this famous ride on the great Five Minutes to Midnight in 1939 at Cheyenne Frontier Days.

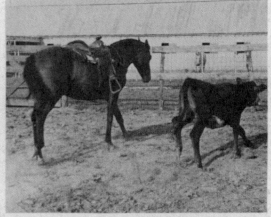

• Charley King used to wow the cutting horse fans with a performance of Jodie Earl, cutting without a rider!

THE WESTERN HORSEMAN

• The grand entry of the Texas High School Championship Rodeo where 12,500 fans watched 213 cowboys and cowgirls compete for a shot at the 6th Annual National High School Championship Rodeo in 1954.

James Cathey Photo

"Daddy of 'em All," dates back to 1897; the Pendleton Round-Up started in 1910; and the Calgary Stampede began in 1912. And the Wild West Shows played a part in history, too—Buffalo Bill, Pawnee Bill, and the famed 101 Ranch Wild West Show being the big ones.

But the rodeo cowboys were never "organized" until they went on strike in the Boston Garden and formed the Cowboys Turtle Association . . . in October 1936! Remember, *The Western Horseman* was already ten months old when this happened.

To follow up the rodeo history, the Turtles didn't become the Ro-

deo Cowboys Association until 1945, in Forth Worth. The association was moved to Denver in 1950, and the name was officially changed to the Professional Rodeo Cowboys Association in 1975.

Now acknowledged and recognized as perhaps the greatest rodeo of all, the National Finals Rodeo held in December each year in Oklahoma City features the top 15 contenders in each event. You have to see this rodeo to believe it. But it got off to a shaky start in 1959 in Dallas. It was held three years in Dallas and three years in Los Angeles before moving to Oklahoma City in 1965. The Oklahoma City move, coordinated with

special events in conjunction with the Cowboy Hall of Fame, seemed to be the shot-in-the-arm it needed; and now sellout crowds are more the rule than the exception in the Jim Norick Arena at the state fairgrounds in Oklahoma City.

Professional rodeo isn't confined only to the PRCA, either. The International Rodeo Association, as we know it today, was formed in 1959. They, too, now have a national finals rodeo each year, which they call the International Finals Rodeo. The first one was held in Tulsa, in 1969, and each year they dub their finals as IFR2, IFR3, etc.

• Casey Tibbs, riding Nugget at Los Angeles in 1954, shows the classic style that made him the measuring-stick for all saddle bronc riders.

R.L. Pound Photo

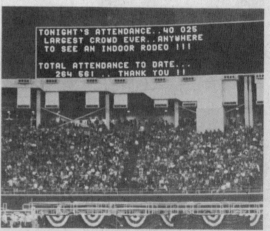

• Started in 1932, the Houston Fat Stock Show moved to the Astrodome in 1966. This record rodeo crowd made history that year.

Ben Allen Photo

• This was the first grand entry of the 1956 rodeo season in the coliseum in Odessa, Texas.

James Cathey Photo

And our good neighbors to the north, where we have thousands of readers, have excellent professional rodeo, too. The Canadian Rodeo Cowboys Association has always maintained the same goals, even though the name has changed several times. They started in July 1944 when rodeo contestants banded together and formed the Canadian Cowboys Insurance Association. This later was changed to the Cowboys Protective Association, and, in 1965, it became known as the Canadian Rodeo Cowboys Association. In 1974 Canada started its own National Finals Rodeo.

Even before the Women's Lib movement got under way, the cowgirls got together and formed the Girls Rodeo Association. It took about a year of groundwork and planning, but in November of 1948 the GRA became a reality in San Angelo, Texas. The following year, 1949, also saw the birth of the National Championship High School Rodeo Association, which came about as a natural outgrowth of the Halletsville (Texas) high school rodeo that started in 1947.

The National Intercollegiate Rodeo Association also started in 1949, in Dallas, with Charlie Rankin of Texas A & M as its first president. That year Sul Ross State won the college team championship, and Harley May was the first NIRA all-around champion cowboy. Then, in June of 1952, Alvin Davis formed the American Junior Rodeo Association after several good junior rodeos had been staged in Texas. The association was started in Levelland. That same year, a Little Britches Rodeo was held at the Arapahoe County Fairgrounds in Littleton, Colorado. It aroused a great deal of interest right from the start, and by January of 1961 the demand for Little Britches rodeos in other states was so great that the National Little Britches Rodeo Association was formed.

• Remember when Jim Shoulders looked like this?

DeVere Photo

• . . . and Casey Tibbs looked like this?

George Baker Photo

• When college rodeo was new, Harley May was the all-around champion. This was his trophy saddle for the second year.

George Baker Photo

THE WESTERN HORSEMAN

• Organized in 1955, the TBRA was proud of this slate of officers in 1958. Front, Velda Smith, Mildred Farris, and NaRay McHood. Standing, Helen Gray, Anna Ruckman, Carolyn Cartwright, and Dathene Vineyard.
James Cathey Photo

• 1949 Girls Rodeo Association champions—Margaret Montgomery, wild cow milking; Amy McGilvray, barrel racing and all-around; Bettye Barron, calf roping; and Jackie Worthington, bareback and bull riding.
James Cathey Photo

Even with the Girls Rodeo Association, another trend was started at Fort Worth in 1955 when the cowgirls organized the Texas Barrel Racers Association. They got it started, and now there are many barrel racing associations for states and regions.

Roping, too, has been around about as long as the cattle industry on this continent; but the history of the big, organized ropings is more recent. The King Merritt Memorial, for instance, was started by King Merritt at Encampment, Wyo., in 1948, and moved to Laramie the following year. It has been known as the King Merritt Memorial since 1953. The Ben Johnson Memorial was started in Pawhuska, Okla., in 1954. California has two of the biggest and most famous ropings—

Oakdale, which has been going since 1956, and Chowchilla, since 1958. And down in Texas, the San Angelo roping dates back to 1954.

Today's cutting horse people owe much to the original group of ranchers and cowboys that got together at Fort Worth in 1946 to form the National Cutting Horse Association. Cutting horses had been around—on ranches and in arenas—but these men brought them into the show window by forming the association, and devising some rules as to how the event should be judged. There have been a lot of great cutting horses, riders, and trainers through the years—but you are already an old-timer if you can remember George Glascock riding Nigger to the first three world championships in 1946, 1947, and 1948. Nigger was

owned by Benny Binion. And in 1949 it was Housekeeper, owned and ridden by Robert Corbett; and the next two years it was Phil Williams and Skeeter.

In 1962 the National Cutting Horse Association established a Cutting Horse Futurity; and, in December of 1975, more than 300 cutting horses were competing for a purse of over $140,000 in Fort Worth. That made this futurity the richest single competition, non-racing horse event in the world.

Each segment of the horse industry has its own history, which is dotted with the names of the stars—the horses and the people—who went down in the record books. This is not intended as a complete history of the last 40 years in the horse business, but

• This was Jackie Worthington about 25 years ago, on Bald Hornet, earning her way into the brand-new Cowgirl Hall of Fame.
James Cathey Photo

• This is the current Denver headquarters for the Professional Rodeo Cowboys Association. Formed in 1945, in Fort Worth, moved to Denver in 1950.

• Painter Orren Mixer did this portrait of Wimpy, the Quarter Horse stallion that earned registry number 1.

• Both of these names will ring a bell with early Quarter Horse enthusiasts: Joe Moore, the horse, and Ott Adams, the man.

perhaps some of the names, dates, places, and events will bring other memories to the fore in your special interest.

Many interested newcomers know that the cherished No. 1 in the AQHA registry went to a horse named Wimpy; but do you all remember that when the studbooks were started, the first 19 numbers were left blank? And this was done on purpose, so that some of the outstanding horses of the times could earn their way into the low numbers. Wimpy, the great King Ranch chestnut stallion, earned the number 1 by winning the grand champion title at the Fort Worth Fat Stock Show in 1941.

Not all phases of the horse industry have exploded with growth and increase. We watched our own

horse cavalry units being phased out and replaced with "tin can cavalry" tank units as our nation girded for war in the early 1940s. And when the "Last of the Best," the two remaining pack mule outfits, were retired from the service on December 15, 1956, *The Western Horseman* was there at Fort Carson, in Colorado, to record the colorful ceremony pictorially.

If you are one of the millions to have visited the Cowboy Hall of Fame in Oklahoma City recently, you might not remember that in the early 1950s it was just a dream to a man named Chester Reynolds. He launched his dream towards reality in the Brown Palace Hotel in Denver, in January of 1955. Plans were set in motion, and various cities bid for the location of the site, and Oklahoma

City got the nod. Ground was broken January 7, 1958, on Persimmon Hill, but it was still a rather sputtering start. Chester Reynolds didn't live to see the results of his dream, but today it is quite a monument to the American cowboy and the pioneers of our west. It was formally dedicated and opened June 26, 1965.

And to show you that things are still happening, and that history is in the making, in August of 1975 a nationwide campaign to raise funds for a National Cowgirl Hall of Fame, to be located in Hereford, Tex., was launched. The first three honorees were named to this hall of fame in 1975—Jackie Worthington of Jacksboro, Tex., Alice Greenough of Tucson, Ariz., and the late Sissy Thurman of Bryan, Texas.

• Bob Denhardt, then editor of *The Western Horseman*, presents the magazine's trophy to George Glascock and Nigger for top cutting horse honors in 1948.

• Two more early day cutters that were always in there with the best: Phil Williams on Skeeter, and Earl Albin on Royal King.
George Baker Photo

Dean Krakel, managing director of the Cowboy Hall of Fame, came up with the idea of forming a Rodeo Historical Society in the spring of 1966. He discussed the idea with George Williams, then editor of *Rodeo Sports News* (which, incidentally, had been started as the official paper of the Rodeo Cowboys Association in November 1952) and they both agreed it was a good idea.

Dean set up a luncheon on December 9, 1966, during the National Finals Rodeo in Oklahoma City. After this meeting, and a following one in January during the R.C.A. convention in Denver, the idea was on the way. Flaxie Fletcher took over the secretarial reins, and it was off and running. Again, *The Western Horseman* helped where we could, even designing the distinctive gold membership pin. Each year, starting in 1967, the Rodeo Historical Society has selected a Rodeo Man of the Year, and we are proud that *The Western Horseman's* Chuck King was presented this award in 1969. Jerry Armstrong, our long-time rodeo reporter, was the first of 35 charter members.

Next let's take a look at trail riding, which is a big corner of the horse interest today. Here, too, there is a "daddy of 'em all." The Rancheros Visitadores ride out of Santa Barbara, Calif., has a rich and colorful history beginning in 1930. This ride is older than *The Western Horseman* magazine, and still going strong. More than that, it was the inspiration for almost all the other "old" trail rides, which began well after *The Western Horseman* was established.

To give you an idea about the history of just a few, Los Caballeros started in 1943; this was another good California ride, which later became famous as the "Catalina ride." The Desert Caballeros ride out of Wickenburg, Ariz., was started by some men in the area as a replacement for the annual Wickenburg Rodeo, and the DC Ride has been a success since the first one in 1947. The Roundup Riders of the Rockies, out of Denver, was started by a group of horsemen returning by plane from the Rancheros Visitadores ride in 1948. Another good Colorado ride was started the following year, in 1949, with the advent of the Pikes Peak Range Ride, to promote the region's annual Pikes Peak or Bust Rodeo.

• In a colorful ceremony at Fort Carson, Colo., the "Last of the Best" paraded into the pages of history in 1956.

• November 11, 1955, saw more than 1,500 horses and riders gathered near Persimmon Hill for the dedication of the National Cowboy Hall of Fame.

• Looking west across the garden pool and memorial walk to the Hall of Great Westerners at the Cowboy Hall of Fame in Oklahoma City.

Some Minnesota horsemen started the Caballeros del Norte in 1953, the same year another good Arizona trail ride was started by the White Mountain Range Riders. The Arizona rides seemed to take hold, and Los Charros Desiertos organized in Tucson in 1956, and the Verde Vaqueros began in 1958 out of Scottsdale. Intermixed in with these dates are many, many more trail rides, but these represent some of the first. California and Arizona undoubtedly have the most organized trail rides in the country, but trail rides are now widely scattered all over the United States. Some for men only, some for women only, and some for whole families.

Trail riding has even gone international in several groups, most noteworthy of which are the Cabalgata rides. These started out with rides in Mexico, and later rides have been held in Ireland, England, Spain, Portugal, and Kenya (Africa) in addition to Hawaii and the Navajo Reservation on the mainland. Many successful trail rides today got their start by running a classified ad in *The Western Horseman*.

The "daddy of the endurance rides" is the Western States 100 Miles in 1 Day Ride, better known as the Tevis Cup Ride. It started in 1955. There were other 100-mile endurance rides, but they were usually three-day rides, and Wendell Robie and his friends didn't feel they really tested the endurance of either horse or rider. After endurance riding was well established, then came the competitive

• Topped by Old Glory, the flags of the 17 western states fly over the National Cowboy Hall of Fame and Western Heritage Center.

THE WESTERN HORSEMAN

• Bill Linderman, "The King," riding Kewpie Doll. *John Stryker Photo*

• Bob Scriver's statue of Bill Linderman, in the Cowboy Hall of Fame.

• Jessie James, with Snooks Burton up, was tough cutting competition in the 1950s. *James Cathey Photo*

trail rides; and in 1971 another race appeared on the scene which is now one of the big "tuffies" of them all—the Levi's Ride and Tie Race! It's an annual event now, and it takes a full year to get your team in shape if you plan to compete.

Back in 1961, the North American Trail Ride Conference had its inception. Its first series of rides culminated that fall in the first annual awards presentations in San Francisco's Cow Palace. Since then many rides have been conducted under the auspices of the

• Pete Knight, the first cowboy name to appear as a Rodeo Hall of Fame honoree.

NATRC, with an eye towards developing uniform rules that will aid management in conducting rides, and enable judges to evaluate each horse on a more objective basis. Each year one horse is named the National Sweepstakes Winner and receives the President's Cup award.

As trail riding began to take on more and more importance on the national scene, in its many variations, we started a column called *Riding The Trails*, which makes it easier for those interested to locate material with this special interest.

In the November 1957 issue we ran an article designed to help youngsters do a better job of showing in horsemanship classes, and the response to this was such that we started working on other related articles. The series ran up into 1959, with letters coming in asking for reprints or back copies of articles that were missed or lost, and we finally came up with the idea of lumping them all into a little book called *Beginning Western Horsemanship*. We didn't expect it to sell well, since the series had just run in the magazine, but the first 10,000 pressrun sold like hotcakes. If you can recall those days, there were very few books on western-style riding available. If you don't remember, look at the publishing dates on some of the great selection of books available

now and see when they came out. In any event, we reordered another printing, and set about putting together other books and working on other series; but this was the beginning of *The Western Horseman* books, and it started a landslide that eliminated the shortage of books on western riding.

In book publishing, many of our titles were "firsts"—they were written because no other books on the subject were available. We published such books as *Calf Roping, Training and Riding the Cutting Horse, Team Roping and Team Tying, Training and Riding the Barrel Horse,* and *Goat Tying*—when no other books on these subjects were available.

• You've got to be an old-timer to recognize these rodeo greats—Burel Mulkey, Hub Whiteman, and Hugh Bennett.

• Roy Barnes staged an early Cuttin' Horse Judges Clinic, country-style, at his Denver arena when cutting horse popularity was spreading.

• Ed Bowman and Sonny Boy could cut cattle in the arena or on the ranch. Ed is another early honoree in the Cowboy Hall of Fame.
Stewart's Photo

• The Pacific Coast Quarter Horse Association was proud of this array of trophies in 1954. West coasters will recognize John Lilley, Ed Tomel, Ralph Howe, Ben Feldman, Wild Bill Elliott, Jim Woodyard, and Bud Anthony.
John Williamson Photo

• Built while the Depression still pinched, people grumbled that money was being spent on a "palace for cows." Completed in 1941, the name Cow Palace stuck, and is now one of the landmarks in San Francisco.

Now, in 1976, we offer 20 titles.

In 1958 *The Western Horseman* won a Maggie Award—which was then to the magazine industry what the Oscar is to motion pictures and the Emmy is to television. We got it for a "how-to series," which was our *Beginning Western Horsemanship* series that launched the book publishing effort. Other Maggie winners that year were *Life, Look, Better Homes and Gardens, Mademoiselle, Good Housekeeping, Sport, Modern Screen,* and *TV Radio Mirror.* A pretty fast track for a little ol' horse magazine!

Another sidelight developed back in 1956 when the Rocky Mountain Quarter Horse Association asked us to work up some sort of "educational program" for free presentation at the 1957 Denver National Western. It sounded like a good idea, and we set to work planning and outlining it. As part of it, we put together a motion picture film . . . color, but no sound. We also shot lots of slides to help in the veterinary part of the presentation. We didn't know what to call the program, but we had heard of photography clinics and writing clinics . . . so we came up with the word "horse clinic." We thought it sounded a little "medical," but we didn't come up with a better word at the time. The first one packed 2,000 people into inadequate space, and we did it again the following year because of the tremendous response. Ed Honnen, a good promoter for the Rocky Mt. Quarter Horse Assn., liked the film idea so well that he instigated the AQHA film pro-

76

• Just about every Quarter Horse fan in the country knew this horse's name and registry number—the great King, P234, owned by Jess Hankins.

• Because of his color, conformation, and the Triangle Bar brand, more people recognized Joker B on sight than any other Appaloosa.

gram shortly after that, only he did it up right! Both sound and color. Other associations followed up on the idea, and now most of them have some sort of film library available for club or individual use. Our original film, with two copies, made the rounds for several years until they just completely wore out. And within a few years there were "clinics" for just about everything—barrel racing, cutting horses, roping, etc.

In 1965 a friend walked in with an idea of using some of our former good covers on a calendar. We liked the idea, selected the covers for it, had to contact each of the artists because we had purchased only one-time rights, and came out with our first *Western Horseman* calendar in 1966. We have published a calendar each year since then, and they have become collectors' items . . . with more people buying them for the western art than for the dates on the calendar.

We're not going to make any claims that we discovered Charlie Russell and Frederic Remington (although we have run lots of their paintings, along with other "old masters" of the west), but most of the top contemporary western artists of today can tell you the month and year their works first appeared in *The Western Horseman*. And when George Phippen, Joe Beeler, John Hampton, and Charlie Dye got together in the Oak Creek Tavern in Sedona, Ariz., and decided to form the Cowboy Artists of America, they sounded us out on the idea. We said to "go to it" and that we'd

give them some publicity. When the article appeared, Johnny Hampton told us ". . . *then came the deluge*!" That was back in 1964. Then, after George Phippen died, and they had their big Cowboy Artists Exhibition at the Cowboy Hall of Fame, we presented the first George Phippen Memorial trophy for the work of art that was most popular in the public's acclaim.

We all know the Thoroughbred and the Arabian are old and well-established breeds, and we know the story of Justin Morgan and his horse, but do you remember that the first national championship classes for Arabians were not held

• Poco Bueno and Pine Johnson. Poco Bueno was one of the greatest sires of his day.   James Cathey Photo

until as late as 1959? Earlier we mentioned the Appaloosa and the Quarter Horse, so let's take a quick look-back in recent history.

In 1937 *The Western Horseman* magazine ran an article about the colorful Appaloosa horses, written by Francis Haines. The interest resulting from this article spurred Claude Thompson of Moro, Ore., into starting a club with others who had these spotted horses—and the Appaloosa Horse Club came into being in December 1938, incorporated under the laws of Oregon. Because of the war years in the interim, progress was relatively slow until the club managed to get out a studbook, and hold its first National Appaloosa Show in 1948, in Lewiston, Idaho.

On March 15, 1940, a meeting was held in Fort Worth to organize the American Quarter Horse Association. Here again, World War II hindered progress in the early years; and the National Quarter Horse Breeders Association got started, causing a split in the early efforts. In 1944 the American Quarter Racing Association was formed, which further complicated the registry systems. It wasn't until 1950 that all agreed on a single registry—the American Quarter Horse Association. Since that time there have been other splits, and other Quarter Horse registries, but the AQHA is still *the* big one, and the largest horse registry in the world.

Racing has been a part of both the Quarter Horse and the Appaloosa heritage, and the All-American Futurity, at Ruidoso Downs, was started in 1959—and is now

• The AQHA building in Amarillo, completed in 1962, and expanded in 1968. The George Phippen statute of Wimpy was donated to the AQHA by the King Ranch.

• The new home of the Appaloosa Horse Club in Moscow, Ida., was dedicated in June of 1974. They just outgrew their old headquarters.

billed as the "richest horse race in the world." The 1975 gross purse was $1,030,000, and the winner collected $330,000. There is also an All-American Derby, for three-year-olds, held at Ruidoso. This Quarter Horse race is the *second* richest race in the world.

The richest Appaloosa race is the Appaloosa World Wide Futurity held during the New Mexico State Fair in Albuquerque. It began in 1962; and, although I didn't win it, I did have a horse that qualified and ran in that first race. The Appaloosa Derby started the next year, and we didn't win that one either, but we were in it. The 1975 winner of the World Wide Futurity received $32,530 of the $81,327 total purse.

Another form of racing that has been around for quite some time, at a regional level, and then suddenly got popular in many other areas, is cutter racing and chariot racing. Of course, the cutter racing was limited to areas where there was sufficient snow, but the little chariots became popular in many places—and other northern states found out this was a thrilling way to have some horse competition in the wintry months.

In 1963 the World Championship Cutter and Chariot Racing Association was organized, and a championship meet was scheduled for each March in Pocatello, Idaho. As of 1975, there were around 30 affiliated associations in this sport, and the AQHA has recognized it for Register of Merit points since 1971.

Some Florida cowboys started a game down there that they called Palmetto Polo, and it was a far cry from the game of polo that most people know. In any event, in 1955 several teams of Texans

put on a round robin exhibition of this new game at the Fort Worth Fat Stock Show. Credit for playing the first organized game of Palmetto Polo goes to the Smyrna Beach Saddle Club of New Smyrna Beach, Florida. And they wrote the rule book for the game. But after its introduction in Texas, at Fort Worth, the game skyrocketed—and was soon known by what the game is called today, *Cowboy Polo*. We ran a story on how to play the game in the May issue of 1955, when it was still called Palmetto Polo.

Back in 1955 the old International Rodeo Association (not to be confused with the new IRA formed in 1959) got the idea of a Miss Rodeo America contest. Herman Linder, John Moss, and Bob Latta gave the idea much study, and came up with a tryout contest in August of 1955 at the Central

• You can't talk about early day Quarter racing for very long without mentioning the great Shue Fly, one of the biggest names on the tracks.

• Mildred Farris of Iowa Park, Tex., was mighty proud of this trophy saddle she won as champion of the Texas Barrel Racers Association for 1957. The TBRA was the first of many barrel racing associations to organize. James Cathey Photo

• **Don Dodge won his share in the 1950s, cutting on Poco Lena.** James Cathey Photo

• **Endurance riders will recognize Nick Mansfield, Will Tevis, and the Tevis Cup.**
Mari Hite Photo

Wyoming Nite Rodeo in Casper. Nineteen queens showed up, eleven for the Wyoming eliminations, and eight from Rocky Mountain states and Canada. Marilyn Scott, then a sophomore at Colorado A & M, won the title of Miss Rodeo America of the Rockies—and this was the beginning of the Miss Rodeo America Pageant.

We have helped in many other ways in the development of the horse industry in the past 40 years—ways in which most people may not realize we helped. A trophy each year to the National Appaloosa Show, for years a saddle to one of the R.C.A. champions, trophies for National Little Britches, buckles for the Girls Rodeo Association, horse judging buckles at the Cow Palace, and countless others to different groups and in different categories. Monetary contributions for the "new" coliseum at the Denver National Western, and to the Cowboy Hall of Fame. Over the years this would make quite a list, but we point it out only because we have been doing it in the background and many people think a magazine's only contribution is through publicity and reporting. And these people may be more right than we are, because in most cases we were the only horse magazine doing this.

Today the Marlboro Man is

about as well-known as any modern cowboy. If you think back, can you remember what he used to look like? Most photos of him were close-up head shots, and he had a tattoo on the back of his hand. He was a "cowboy," but he didn't look like a real cowboy. Anyway, a *Western Horseman* advertising manager, Clarence Colbert, had Randy Steffen make a painting to show what a modern cowboy looked like. This painting went back to the agency that handled the Marlboro account, and hung in their offices for a long time. Shortly after that the real "Marlboro Man" evolved, and they went from models to real cowboys. They did such a good job, *The Western Horseman* magazine presented them with a trophy for their portrayal of the contemporary cowboy back in 1967. And we don't even accept tobacco advertising. It was just something we wanted to do, for some people who had done an outstanding job.

For 40 years *The Western Horseman* has been a part of this growth. The magazine has lived it, grown along with it, and participated—perhaps even more than many readers would realize, or expect. Our main job, of course, is to report—to inform, to entertain, and to make it interesting. From the beginning it was felt that to do this right, we must participate. True, a good journalist should be

able to put out a good horse magazine and not even own a horse, or ride. But we can't, and don't, rely on that.

We have always felt that we, too, should experience firsthand the "thrill of victory and the agony of defeat." We have the same gut-feelings you have when we have an orphaned foal, or a sick horse, or the price of feed skyrockets. We have to worry about fencing, and stabling, and trailering, and shoeing, and vet bills, and feed—and the budget.

We can appreciate firsthand the problems of the horse owner, the breeder, the rancher, the horse show exhibitor, the rodeo cowboy, the trail rider, the packer, and the

• **In 1967 *The Western Horseman* presented a special trophy at the Pikes Peak or Bust Rodeo to the Philip Morris Tobacco Company and the Leo Burnett Agency for the creation of the "Marlboro cowboy" ads. Rancher Bob Norris, one of the early Marlboro models, was there for the ceremony.**

• Hard Twist had an easy number to remember, P5555. He was a handsome horse to look at, and his name still looks good in a pedigree.

• A Thoroughbred horse named Three Bars put the "Bar" name indelibly into the Quarter Horse breed. This is Art Pollard's Lightning Bar.
Matt Culley Photo

pleasure rider. And we are not a "one-breed" staff, either. Today, at this moment, our staff members have Quarter Horses, Thoroughbreds, Arabians, Appaloosas, and a number of just good grade horses and ponies. At various other times in the past we have had many other breeds, too, so our interests and leanings are not slanted in any one direction.

A magazine is expected to "report"—but not all magazines participate in what they report. We feel this gives a better insight to the reader. Our staff members *go* on the roundups, the brandings, the cattle drives, the trail rides, the pack trips, and to the horse shows, the sales, the conventions, the rodeos—in short, anything that we think will make good reading in the magazine. No horse magazine can have a staff that can

make them all, and we can't either. But no other horse magazine has even come close in all-around participation reporting.

We buy material, too. This gives every reader a chance to become part of the overall tone and direction of the magazine. Some are professional writers with the training and know-how to have many stories sold; some are from people with little journalistic training, but with an interesting story to tell.

For years and years we carried a column in the magazine called *Drifting,* and it was filled with many little items too brief for a special article. Into this column fell the items that were newly manufactured for the horse or horseman. In June of 1959 we started sending a special newsletter called *Western Preview* to

manufacturers and retailers interested in what was new in the field of western wear and gear. This area of coverage was growing so fast in those days that we started carrying this material as a column in the magazine in June of 1961. Prior to our *Western Preview* newsletter there was nothing going directly to these specialized manufacturers and retailers; and then, in 1960, the first "trade journal" (called *Western Wear & Equipment*) appeared on the scene. Now there are several trade journals in this field alone.

Before 1966 the western apparel and equipment manufacturers were all busily engaged in making and selling equipment to horse owners, but there was no cohesion. They suddenly realized they had mutual interests, and in January of 1966 they formed WAEMA—

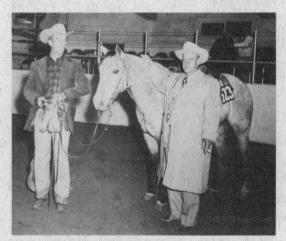

• E. Paul Waggoner and his horses were prominent in Quarter Horse circles. Here is E. Paul and the great Snipper W, with rider Pine Johnson.
James Cathey Photo

• More names you might remember—Go Man Go, a son of Top Deck, was sold by A.B. Green to John B. Ferguson for $40,200 for a new record price in 1956.

GARCIA SADDLERY CO.

Manufacturers of the Finest

SADDLES ♦ HARNESS

Silver Mounted

BITS & SPURS
♦
Silver Work

Our Specialty

Stores Located At

10 W. Gabilan St.   Elko,
Salinas, Calif.   Nevada

• An ad from the first issue, 1936.

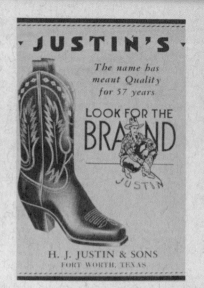

JUSTIN'S

The name has
meant Quality
for 57 years

LOOK FOR THE
BRAND

H. J. JUSTIN & SONS
FORT WORTH, TEXAS

• Justin boots advertised with us in 1936,
and still do today.

many, many times before—in the magazine, in letters, and in talking with people. We have long maintained a 50-50 percentage ratio of ads to editorial material. When you see more ads in the magazine, it doesn't mean "there's nothing in it but ads." It means you also have more *editorial* material. Every issue is measured, *by inches,* and that 50-50 ratio is very close. We *have* to know, because our postal rates are determined on this advertising-editorial percentage. If one issue is a bit lopsided by a percentage point or two, we make it up in another issue. So when you see an issue with 200 pages in it, you can bet that about 100 pages of it are editorial; and this has been true since the magazine averaged 48 pages an issue back about 25 years ago.

Forty years of advertising in the magazine tells a story, too. Some names from Volume 1 are still around, and a good many others are not. Garcia, Justin, Visalia, and Cutter Laboratories are names you still see around—and there are many you would recognize, but they are not as prominent today.

Levi Strauss came west with the California gold-seekers, and John B. Stetson made his first hat in the shadow of Pikes Peak during the "Rush to the Rockies"—also for gold. In the history of the west, *Levi's* came to mean pants, and *Stetson* came to mean hat. Both of these names appeared in ads in the first issue of *The Western Horseman.*

The "big name" saddles of the 1940s and '50s are not the big name saddles of today; even

which is what those letters stand for, Western Apparel and Equipment Manufacturers Association.

In the early 1950s the horse boom was on for real, and we singled out our May issue in 1953 for a special issue on western wear and equipment. It has been an annual event every year since, and now almost every horse magazine has such a special issue—as well as a column devoted to new products. Fortunately, as we grew in size, we have been able to keep a large percentage of that issue devoted to good horse articles in addition to the "fashion book" image; but this was not easy to do in the early years when we didn't have the pages to work with.

And right here I'd like to reiterate something we have said

though many of the saddles are still being ridden, and some of them are still being made. We won't go into that in depth, because the story of saddles tells its own interesting story of the west. At one time or another, most all of the saddlemakers of renown appeared in print in *The Western Horseman.*

The most advanced developments in horse feed nutrients and nutriments unfolded in the pages of the magazine; along with medicines, veterinary practices, and health care products. We reported such names as Toots Mansfield, Paul Bond, Gerald Roberts, and Jim Shoulders when they were rodeo greats—and then followed them through into other fields of endeavor, such as roping

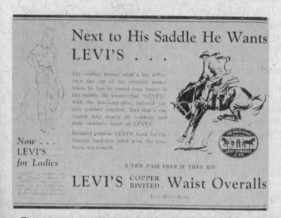

Next to His Saddle He Wants
LEVI'S . . .

Now . . .
LEVI'S
for Ladies

A NEW PAIR FREE IF THEY RIP

LEVI'S COPPER RIVITED Waist Overalls

BLACKLEGOL . . .

An entirely different,
more potent vaccine . . .
guaranteed to produce
a greater immunity than
any bacterin or aggressin
on the market (including our own).

10 cents per full 5 c.c. dose — Less in quantities

CUTTER LABORATORIES
Established 1867   Berkeley, California

• These two companies have "grown up with the west" and have been advertising with *The Western Horseman* since 1936.

and rodeo schools, stock contracting, and the manufacturing of boots, rodeo equipment, and other equipment, and other western items. These are but a few of the early ones; now there are many.

The first issue carried a number of little one-inch ads—Betty Ross Coffee Shop in Walnut Creek; Stone's Shoe Repair Shop in Berkeley; Walsh's Pharmacy in Concord; Concord Mercantile Co. Hay and Feed; Atlas Tires and Batteries at Gean's Service Station; and Davis Auto Exchange ("we make horse trailers")—and quite a few others. Levi Strauss had the top half of the inside front cover, and P.L. Castro, wholesale butcher of Richmond, Calif., had the bottom half. The back cover went to Cutter Laboratories, and Pacific Molasses Co., with Hawaiian Cane-Feed Molasses . . . one of the "best horse feeds known."

As the years progressed, other names cropped up: H Bar C, Tony Lama, Keyston, H.D. Lee, Visalia, Heiser, N. Porter, Mueller, Miller, Nocona, Hamley's, Hyers. And then more names, like Blue Bell Wranglers, Acme, Miley, Bailey, Resistol, Farnam, Merck, Longhorn, Big Horn, Simco. . . .

As you read the names, perhaps you can recall their ads and the products they made or sold. Names like Bona Allen, Tex Tan, Ozark, Durango, Texas, Blucher, Frye, Sanders, Lasso, Panhandle Slim, Prior, Karman, Tem Tex, Dickson-Jenkins, Stidham, Merhow, Lincoln Steel, Imperial, Haynes, Hale.

Does this stir up memories? And how about Moore, and American Hats, and the "Leddy bunch," and Johnson halters, and Stockmen's, and Diamond? What do such names as Ryon's, Luskey's, Kauffman, Eddie Bauer, and Eiser's mean to you? And how do these names fit into the horse picture . . . Carnation-Albers, Shell, Absorbine, Ralston-Purina, and Allied Mills?

You can make up your own game of "remember the name" by going through back issues of *The Western Horseman.* Kelly, Crockett, Quick, Sliester, Ortega . . . and on through a long, long line. What did they make? What did they sell? Where are they today? It's quite a game, and they all

played a part in the past 40 years of the horse business, and in the history of this magazine.

Advertising plays a vital role. Not only in the magazine, but in the entire horse industry. It lets horse people know what products are available, and it reflects the leading edge of ideas for *new* products for the horse or horseman. In this way, ads are informative, too.

Nowadays, as a trend of the times, every magazine has to have a survey to "know their readers." It's the smart, businesslike thing to do, and we have just completed a brand new survey for 1975. But even before this, we felt we must "know our readers." We have made it a point to talk to people—at conventions, banquets, sales, shows, rodeos, and on ranches, rides, roundups, and pack trips. And we read every letter that comes in. But long before this we ran our first survey; back when horse magazines were pretty scarce, and we had never heard of a horse magazine making a survey before. Our first one went out in the April 1949 issue. Our second one went into every copy of the July 1952 issue. Surveys *do* help any magazine to get a better overall picture of who buys the magazine, and we do appreciate all the readers who have helped us.

In comparatively recent years horse magazines have sprouted and flourished like wildflowers after the spring rains. In earlier days, they sprouted—but many withered on the vine and died. Not all of them were bad, either. Some were good, and well-edited—but were simply "before the time was ripe." Today there is sufficient horse interest to warrant several horse magazines, in addition to the very necessary breed journals.

This is a highly competitive market, this horse magazine business; but I believe you would find no one in the horse magazine business, either among those now flourishing or those that died, who would accuse us of using shady tactics in competition. We have

devoted much more time to helping competitors out than to backbiting them. There are still "oldtimers" around who might remember that we showed the founders of the *Quarter Horse Journal* everything we knew about putting out a magazine . . . editorial, advertising, and circulation. And the *Appaloosa News* can and will tell you how we helped them over the years, even before they had a newsletter. Other magazines, too; but it is possible that this is of interest only to them, and us.

We are, and have been for some time, the largest-circulation horse magazine in the world. Recently one of our friendly competitors has made a big issue of having "the largest *subscription* circulation" of any horse magazine, and this is true. We had, and still have, the opportunity to gain subscription circulation the same way; but since *The Western Horseman* is our *only* business, and our only magazine, we have never made any "special deals" for either circulation or advertising. We depend upon natural growth in these areas; and circulation, whether by subscription or on the newsstand, has to carry its own weight. We believe in selling magazines, not buying readers. *Collier's, Liberty, Saturday Evening Post, Life,* and a good many others learned long ago you can't have advertisers paying for the whole package. When advertising drops off, we still have to put out a product, and the people who buy *The Western Horseman* help us pay for that product. It takes the income from both advertising and circulation to allow us to continue to operate the way we do.

Whether you buy *The Western Horseman* on the newsstand or subscribe to it, the end result is the same. More people buy *The Western Horseman* each month than any other horse magazine in the world.

Well, we've skipped through the last 40 years of the western horse business pretty rapidly. Not necessarily in chronological order, and far from completely, but you can readily see that it has been a vital and energetic four decades. And we were part of it, and are looking forward to a future that is just as vital and energetic. We hope that you, too, will find it interesting. 🐎

INDEX

A

Albert, Paul, 4, 9–17, 24, 123
Albert, Worth, 9–11, 12, 14, 17, 123
Albino Horse Club, 15
Alfredo, Don (Father Rivard), 15
Allan, Jim, 15
American Paint Horse Association, 130
American Quarter Horse Association
    (AQHA), 15, 25, 29
Anderson, Bert, 107, 110
Appaloosa Horse Club, 15, 130
Armstrong, Jerry, 65, 76
Arnold, Darrell, 100, 108
Audit Bureau of Circulations, 114
Augusta Cutting Horse Futurity, 126–27

B

Baker, Susie (Morris), Lee, and children,
    125, 126, 127
Baratono, Tony, 88
Barber, Howard, 26, 41, 57, 62, 64, 68
Barnes, Jake, 117
Barrel Horse News, 124
Barrett, Hadley, 112
Barton, Herb, 108, 111, 121
Beeby, George, 21
Beeby, Harry, 21, 23
Beeler, Joe, 65
Beginning Western Horsemanship
    (Spencer), 45, 46, 76, 95
Benson, Cade and Mona, 102
Bergen, Chandler W. "Chan"
    background, 54–57
    and Harry Bunker's death, 57–59
    marriage, 56
    photos, 52, 54, 55, 56, 60, 73, 75
    and *Western Horseman* magazine, 5, 6, 57,
        59, 64, 65, 68, 70, 73, 79, 81, 83, 84, 86, 88,
        96, 98, 104, 108, 111, 112
Bergen, Melitta (Niitsoo), 56, 59, 88
Betts, Mona, 51
Black, Baxter, 104, 118
Blaine, Hugh, 56–57
Bloom, Lynda, 88
Bonge, Ron, 132
Bonham, Biddy and Wayne, 86
Bottoms, Joe, 116

Brech, Dwayne, 67, 76, 99, 100, 101, 109
Brown, Barbara, 88
Brown, Freckles, 5
Bumgardner, Hal, 59, 61, 64, 70, 73, 82, 96
Bunker, Harry S., 27, 31, 47, 57–59, 104
Bushey, Ellen, 61, 64

C

Cage, Claude, 102
Calf Roping (Cooper), 92, 93
Camarillo, Jerold, 95
Camarillo, Leo, 92, 93, 95, 117
Camarillo, Reg, 95
Carrel, Charlie, 84
Cater, Marilee, 61, 64
Circuit, Jeff, 100
Close, Patricia A. "Pat"
    background, 51
    horsemanship, 51–53
    photos, 50, 52, 53, 60, 61, 108
    and *Western Horseman* magazine, 51, 52,
        64, 82, 86, 95, 98, 102, 104, 108, 115, 116,
        117, 120–21
Clymer, Sarah, 87
Coalson, Carol, 110, 117
Coalson, Jenny, 117
Cocroft, Larraine, 110
Colbert, Clarence, 19, 25, 26, 30, 49
Colorado Springs' Pioneers Museum, 60
Connelly, Barbara, 64
Conrad, Paul, 37
Cook, Bobbie, 135
Coolidge, Dan, 15
Cooper, Clay O'Brian, 117
Cooper, Roy, 92, 93, 95
Cow Palace, 76
Craig, Mike, 95

D

Darnell, Greg, 116
Davis, Ray, 41, 43, 65
Dean, Graham, 19
Denhardt, Robert "Bob," 14–16, 25–26,
    27–29
Denhardt, Sarah, 25–26
Denison, Jennifer, 131, 136
Denver, John, 49

Denver International Western/English
    Apparel & Equipment Market, 70
Denver Merchandise Mart, 70
Dobbin, Cecil, 67
Dobie, J. Frank, 29
Dodds, Al, 130
Dodds, Darrell, 4, 102, 103, 108, 129–31, 136
Dunning, Al, 52, 92, 93, 95
Dusard, Jay, 86
Dye, Charlie, 65

E

*Editorial Cartooning, the Techniques and
    Tricks of the Trade* (Spencer), 37
Ehringer, Gavin, 100
El Paso County Horsemen's Council, 52
Emerson, Barbara, 5, 60, 64
Engel-Currin, Rayanne, 133
Equi-Stat, 127

F

Feick, Bill, 21
Fenwick, Red, 6
Fernimen, Marge, 25, 26
Flint, Don
    death of, 104
    and the Flying Horse Ranch, 41
    photos, 25, 49
    and *Western Horseman* magazine, 19–21,
        25–29, 31, 41, 59
Flint, Florence, 19, 29, 41, 59, 104

G

Gaffney, Merrill, 19
Games on Horseback, 57
Gibson, Penny, 111, 117
Girls Rodeo Association, 76
Glendenning, George, 15
Goodwin, Brenda, 115
Great Basin, 85–86, 93
Great Depression, 9, 33
Grenier, Jeanne, 21–22

H

Haines, Francis, 15
Halliday, Dick, 15
Hampton, John, 65
Harris, John, 38, 59, 61, 64, 70, 75, 78, 96
Hatley, George, 44
Head, Jeffrey, 22
Head, Maurice, 21, 22
Hecox, Ross, 136–37
Helfrich, Devere, 57
Hewitt, Bob, 88

Hickey, Dolores, 112, 118–19
Hoffman, Pat, 64, 82–83
Holmes, Frank, 115, 117, 136
Holst, Jack, 108, 112
Holt, Deanna, 110
Honnen, Ed, 76
Horse Breaking (Spencer), 47, 77
Horsecity.com, 124
horse clinics, 76
Horseman and Fair World, 29
Horseman's Scrapbook, 47
Horsemen's Yankee Pedlar, 124
Houston, Jim, 5
Hughes, Chuck, 104
Hughes, Mack, 88
Hughes, Stella, 88, 89
Hunt, Ray, 128, 136
Hurley, Jimmie, 88

I

Imprint Training (Miller), 90
Ingles, Hugh, 87
International Finals Rodeo, 76

J

JBS, A Biography of John Ben Snow
    (Snow), 20
Jennings, Jim, 102, 103
John Ben Snow Foundation, 73

K

Kadash, Kathy. *See* Swan, Kathy
Karaban, Bruce, 100
Karaban Labiner and Associates, 100
Keeney, Bob, 12, 17
Keilers, Helen, 109, 117
Kendrick, Ruth, 62, 64
King, Charles G. "Chuck"
    background, 53–54
    death of son, 73
    horsemanship, 54, 76
    photos, 52, 54, 60
    and the *Quarter Horse News,* 28
    and *Western Horseman* magazine, 52, 54,
        59, 64, 65, 67, 68, 70, 73–75, 76, 96
King, Ernie, 116, 131
King, Mac, 54, 73
King, Margaret, 54, 73, 96
Kit Carson Trail Riding Club, 78
Koht, E. Rodney "Rod," 26–27, 49, 57, 59,
    64, 65, 70, 96–98
Koht, Helen, 98
Komatz, Gwen, 62, 64, 82
Kuehn, Kay, 62, 64

L

Lafayette Horse Show, 12
Langmore, Bank, 86
Laughlin, Mike, 88, 101, 119
Laughlin, Pat, 119
Lavelett, Ralph, 41, 63, 64, 84
Lawson, Sanders, 133
Lea, Tom, 29
Leaveck, LiAnne, 111
Lightfoot, Morgan, 102, 103
Lowery, Chuck, 64

M

Major, Mike, 117
Maloney, J., 23
Mangum, A. J., 117, 135, 136
March & McCarty, 64
Mariani, John, 29
Markus, Debra Jean "Debbie" (Spencer),
    31, 37, 44, 82, 88, 96
Markus, Ian Nevada and Westin
    Montana, 98
Markus, Jessica Jo "Jade," 96, 98
Markus, Kurt, 75, 80, 82, 83, 85–86, 88,
    93–96, 98, 100
Markus, Maria, 96
Marquez, Bob, 62, 64, 65
Marshall, Bart, 64, 65, 98, 107, 108
Mattingly, Glenn, 110
May, Pete, 124
Mazerall, Jeanne, 109
McLaury, Buster, 88
Merrick, Walter, 117
Merritt, Hyde, 25, 27, 28–29
Merritt, King, 29
Miller, Karan, 111
Miller, Mitch, 132
Miller, Robert M., 65, 88, 90
Minor, Helen, 15
Mixer, Orren, 29
Morgan, Butch, 108, 112–14, 115, 117,
    118–20, 132
Morgan, Charlene, 112–13, 132
Morgan, Christy, 117
Morris, Caroline, Will, and children, 125
Morris, Mary Sue "Sissie" (Ellis),
    125, 126
Morris, Tyler, 125, 126
Morris, William S. II, 125, 126
Morris, William S. III "Billy," 122, 124–29
Morris Communications Company, 121,
    124, 126, 127, 131
Mueller, Bill and Eleanor, 49
Munson, Pat, 63, 64

N

National Appaloosa Show, 76
National Barrel Horse Association, 127
National Cowboy Hall of Fame, 76
National Finals Rodeo, 76
National Little Britches, 76
National Western Stock Show, 70, 76
Nelson, Barney, 88
Newman, Marty, 130
Niemeyer, Time, 121
Niemeyer, Trey, 87, 121

O

Ortega, Luis B., 15, 29

P

Palmer, Corliss, 77, 78–79, 108, 109
Palmer, Gen. William Jackson, 25
Palmer, Scott, 111
Palomino Horse Association, 15
Pate, Curt, 117
Peavy, Marshall and Mavis, 90
Pennington, Bill, 75, 102, 107, 108, 112
Performance Horse Sales Price Guide, 127
Peterson, Kami and Shane, 134
Petrenas, Marilyn, 110
Phippen, George, 29, 65, 71, 79, 121
Pierce, Sharon, 63, 64
Pierson, Robert R., 64
Pikes Peak Range Riders, 47, 57, 58, 104
Pinell, Jeanette, 62, 64
Poston, Dwaine, 98
Prentice, Steve, 61, 64
Prewitt, Bob, 67
Professional Rodeo Cowboys
    Association, 6
Pulitzer Prize Cartoons (Spencer), 37

Q

Quarter Horse News, (King), 28–29
Quarter Horse News, (Morris), 124, 127
Quinlan, Julie, 111

R

Raine, Lee, 88, 119
Rancheros Visitadores, 76
Raney, C.P., 12
Rayford, Irene, 26, 61, 64, 83
Reining (Dunning), 92, 93
Riding and Training for the Show Ring, 51
Roberds, Coke, 27
Roberts, Ed, 130
Rocky Mountain Quarter Horse
    Association, 76

Rodeo Cowboys Association, 6, 76
Rodeo Historical Society, 76
Rodeo Pictures, 57

S

Sanders, Jenn, 133
Sartin, Roy Jo, 117
Schirra, Wally, 49, 104
Schoner, Ruth, 65
Schutts, Carol, 110
Scribner, Glen, 59
Serpa, Louise, 120
Sheppard, Bill, 130
Shepperdson, Eleanor, 63, 64
Simshauser, Kim, 110
Skalla, John, 104
Skorpinski, Peg, 9–11, 14
Smith, Dorothy, 11, 13, 15
Smith, Fran, 115–17, 135
Snow, John Ben "JBS"
    death of, 73
    early life and education, 20
    and Flying Horse Ranch, 41–44
    and F.W. Woolworth Co., 19–21
    and Highfield Stud Farm, 21–24
    horsemanship, 21, 47
    later years, 59
    management style, 20
    photos, 20, 23, 24, 32, 48
    Speidel Inc. and *Western Horseman,* 17,
        19–20, 25, 26–27, 59, 70
Snow, Vernon F., 20–22, 44
Snow Family Trust, 73
Snow Memorial Trust, 73
Snyder, John, 6
Speidel, Merritt C., 21, 22–24, 25, 27
Spencer, Barbara Jo "Bobbi Jo," 36–38,
    44–45, 46, 47, 88, 91
Spencer, Bill, 32, 33
Spencer, C.R. and Jessie, 32–33
Spencer, Debbie. *See* Markus, Debra
    Jean
Spencer, Dick, III
    after the war, 36–37
    background and education, 32–38
    and cartooning, 29, 36, 37, 49, 97
    death and funeral, 104
    and Harry Bunker's death, 57–59
    horsemanship, 44–45, 47–48
    as a jokester, 48–49, 82–84
    marriages and divorce, 34, 96
    photos, 30, 32, 33, 34, 37, 38, 39, 45, 47,
        48, 49, 58, 60, 75, 87, 102, 105
    as a teacher, 37

and *Western Horseman* magazine, 3, 4, 5,
    6, 19, 29, 31–32, 52, 54, 56–57, 59, 64–68,
    73. 75–76, 79, 81, 83–84, 76, 93, 95, 98,
    100, 102, 107, 108–9, 116
    and World War II, 34–36
    as a writer, 35, 37, 45, 47
Spencer, JoAnne (Nicholson), 31, 33–35,
    36–37, 47, 49, 96
Spencer, R.E. and Nettie, 33
Spencer, Richard Craig "Rick," 37, 44, 73
Spencer, Vivian (King), 96, 102, 108
Stees, Mike and Mary, 90
Steffen, Randy, 29, 45, 47
stock horse competitions, popularity of, 4
Stout, Charles H., 27
Stout, Dave, 6
Streeter, Dan, 136
Swan, Kathy (Kadash), 115
Swan, Rick, 109, 115

T

Team Roping (Camarillo), 92, 93
Thomson, Donald B., 64
Thorson, Juli, 87, 117–18

U

Upchurch, Warren, 111

V

Van Cleve, Spike, 27
Varoz, Ernie, 111
Vollrath, Bill, 63, 64
Vorhes, Corliss. *See* Palmer, Corliss
Vorhes, Gary W.
    and Butch Morgan, 118–19
    divorce, 78–79
    photos, 77, 115, 119
    and polo, 117
    and *Western Horseman* magazine,
        77–78, 79, 100, 121
Vorhes, Tara and Amy, 77, 78, 79, 117

W

Walker, Linda, 102–4
Westerbuhr, Corliss A. *See* Palmer,
    Corliss
Western Horseman magazine
    and the A.B. Hirschfeld Press, 47, 70
    advertising and editorial departments,
        67, 68–73, 100
    age of technology and electronic
        production, 4, 100, 123–24
    books, 45–47, 57, 92, 93, 95, 116–18
    calendars, 94, 95

changing demographics, 130
covers and Western art, 40, 66, 70, 71, 76, 99, 101, 104
development of the horse industry, 76
and Facebook, 131
founding of, 5, 9–17, 24
freelancers, 67–68, 88–90
horsebreeds and breed registries, 13–14
and International Circulation Distributors, 41, 100
mistakes made through the years, 100
move to Colorado Springs, 18, 20
newsstands and retail stores, 114
and Speidel Newspapers Inc., 17, 21, 26, 59
stocks, 27, 108–9, 121
as a successful magazine, 4, 12
travel and art, 86–88
and World Color Press, 100
into the 21st century, 123–37
in the 1950's, 41–49
in the 1960's, 51–65
in the 1970's, 66–79
1976 reprint, Dick Spencer, 138–53
in the 1980's, 93–105
in the 1990's, 106–21

Western riding, as an international pursuit, 4
White, Joyce, 88
Wiescamp, Hank, 86, 117
Wiese, Cory, 131, 134
Wise, Jim, 5
Witte, Marsha (Stees), 5, 79, 84, 87, 88–90, 101, 104, 113, 118, 121
Witte, Mary Claire, 79, 84, 87–90, 104, 113, 117, 121
Witte, Randy
    as author of this book, 4–6
    career at *Western Horseman,* 4–6, 68, 79–81, 84, 86, 88–90, 98, 100, 102, 104, 108, 112–15, 116, 118, 120–21
    college, 4–5
    as a newspaper reporter, 6
    photos, 82, 87, 88, 103, 108, 120
    as rodeo publicist, 5
Wood, Don, 96, 98, 100, 108, 109
Wood, Rick, 100
Wood, Zack T., 124

Y
Yates, J.D., 85
Young, Joe de, 29

AUTHOR PROFILE: RANDY WITTE

Randy Witte worked for *Western Horseman* magazine from 1977 through 2006, starting as editorial assistant and progressing through roles as associate editor, editor, and finally publisher beginning in 1989. In celebration of the magazine's 75th anniversary, he wrote a history of *Western Horseman* that is filled with colorful profiles of the owners, editors and writers who have informed and entertained generations of readers and riders ever since 1936.

From the beginning, *Western Horseman* was there to encourage the formation of various breed associations and registries, and to help readers learn how to raise, train, care for, and use their horses. This book is filled with photos, personal recollections, and vignettes of the people who helped to shape the magazine and see the horse re-emerge as an important part of the American West.

Today, Randy and his wife, Marsha, still have horses, and they also raise Longhorn cattle east of Colorado Springs. During the course of 50 years, Randy went from being a *Western Horseman* reader to longtime staff member and now is back to being a dedicated reader of his favorite magazine.

The author was honored in 2007 at the National Cowboy Symposium in Lubbock, Texas, when he was presented with the American Cowboy Culture Award for Western Writing and Publishing.

COURTESY ALVIN DAVIS